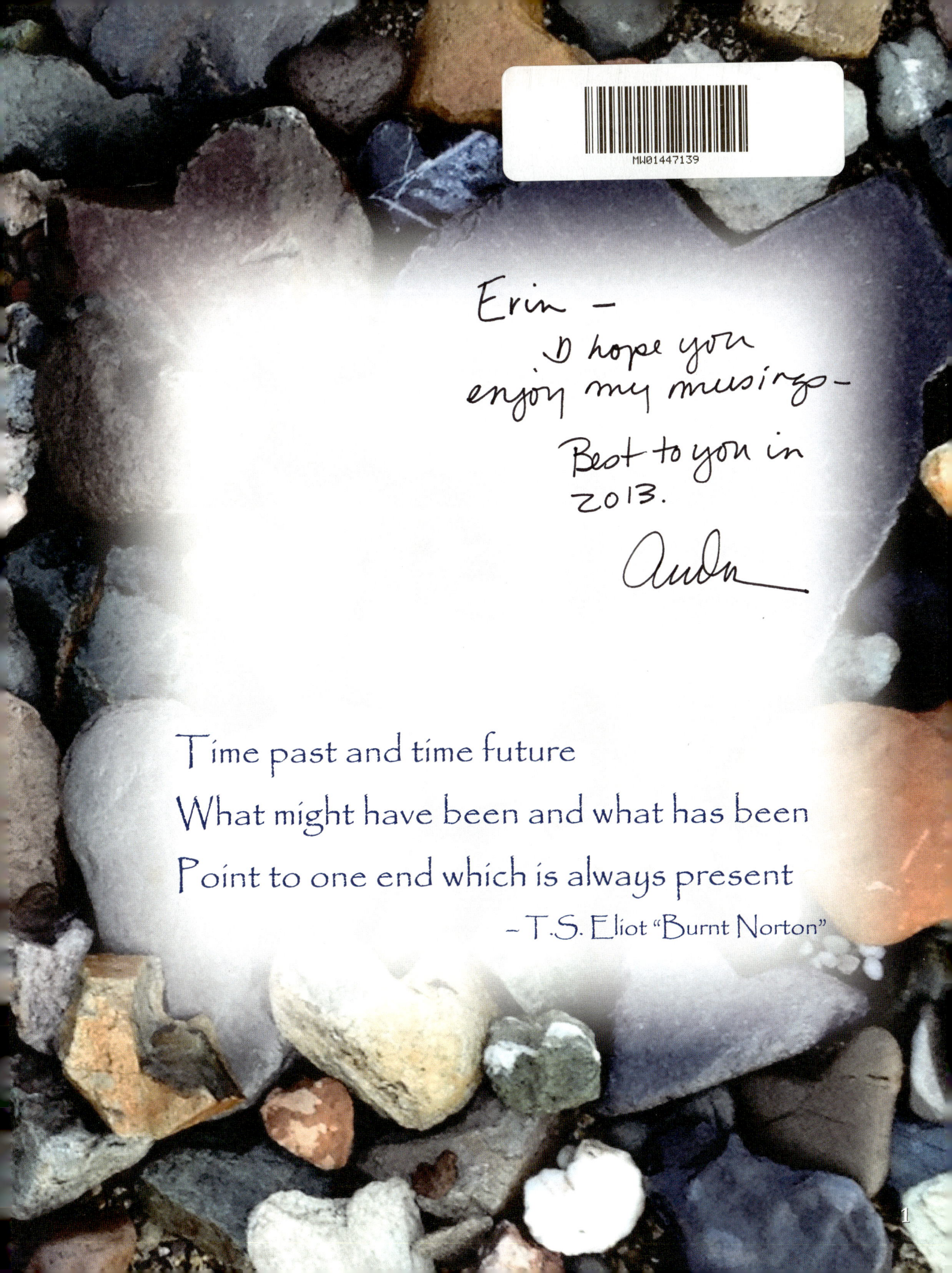

Erin —
I hope you enjoy my musings —
Best to you in 2013.

Time past and time future
What might have been and what has been
Point to one end which is always present
— T.S. Eliot "Burnt Norton"

About this Collection

At the beginning of 2012, I was asked to write a weekly blog for an online community, spiritedwoman.com.

This book is a collection of many of those posts, whose central theme is relationship. I have sought to build upon the relationships we enjoy with ourselves, with key others and our animal companions, as well as that oh-so-important relationship we have with time – the present moment at hand – as that is where the magic of a purposeful life begins.

The common denominator that defines my work is the connection we have or seek, and connection is a primal need. That's why there's so much distress in organizations when personal agendas and misplaced hierarchical boundaries trump inclusion and collaboration. It's why, in one-on-one relationships, we seek to be heard and understood first and foremost. The basis of trust is the feeling that one is safe with the other – and trust is required for engagement of any kind. Perhaps most important is a connection with ourselves; an eyes-wide-open type of awareness that stems from honest self-examination and leads to two things: a state of being called "settled in self," as well as on-purpose action.

As you read my musings, consider your own. There's plenty of space to make this your personal journal. And I invite you to begin a dialogue with those in your circle. Share your own stories and reflections to spread the spirit of connection among all of us.

©2012 Andrea Chilcote

This Very Moment, by Andrea Chilcote, is copyrighted material. All rights reserved. Except for use in a review, no portion of this book may be reproduced mechanically, electronically or by any other means, including photocopying, now known or hereafter invented without written permission of the publisher.

ISBN: 978-0-9882927-1-0

Morningstar Ventures, Inc.
P.O. Box 1723 – Cave Creek, AZ 85327
www.morningstarventures.com

Printed in the United States of America
First Printing October, 2012
10 9 8 7 6 5 5 3 2 1

Contents

Being Here Now 4
Which Story Are You Telling? 8
What Is Your Anchor? 12
The Year of Your Heart's Desire 16
Love In The Midst Of Loss 20
Mirror Mirror 24
It's How You Play the Game 28
A Week Full of Grace 32
My Left Leg 36
What I Control 40
Becoming the Change 44
It Took A Village 48
I Just Assumed… 52
Heart-Inspired Action 56
Still, I Learn 60
The "Nothing" That is Everything 64
A Pack of Friends or One at a Time? 68
Putting Self First 72
Letting Go 76
Living Through It 80
Transform Judgment 84
Who Are You? 88
The Need for Renewal 92
The Personal Plus of Positive Intent 96
Transition's Destination 100
The Story of This Very Moment 104
Just Chill 108
We See What We Expect 112

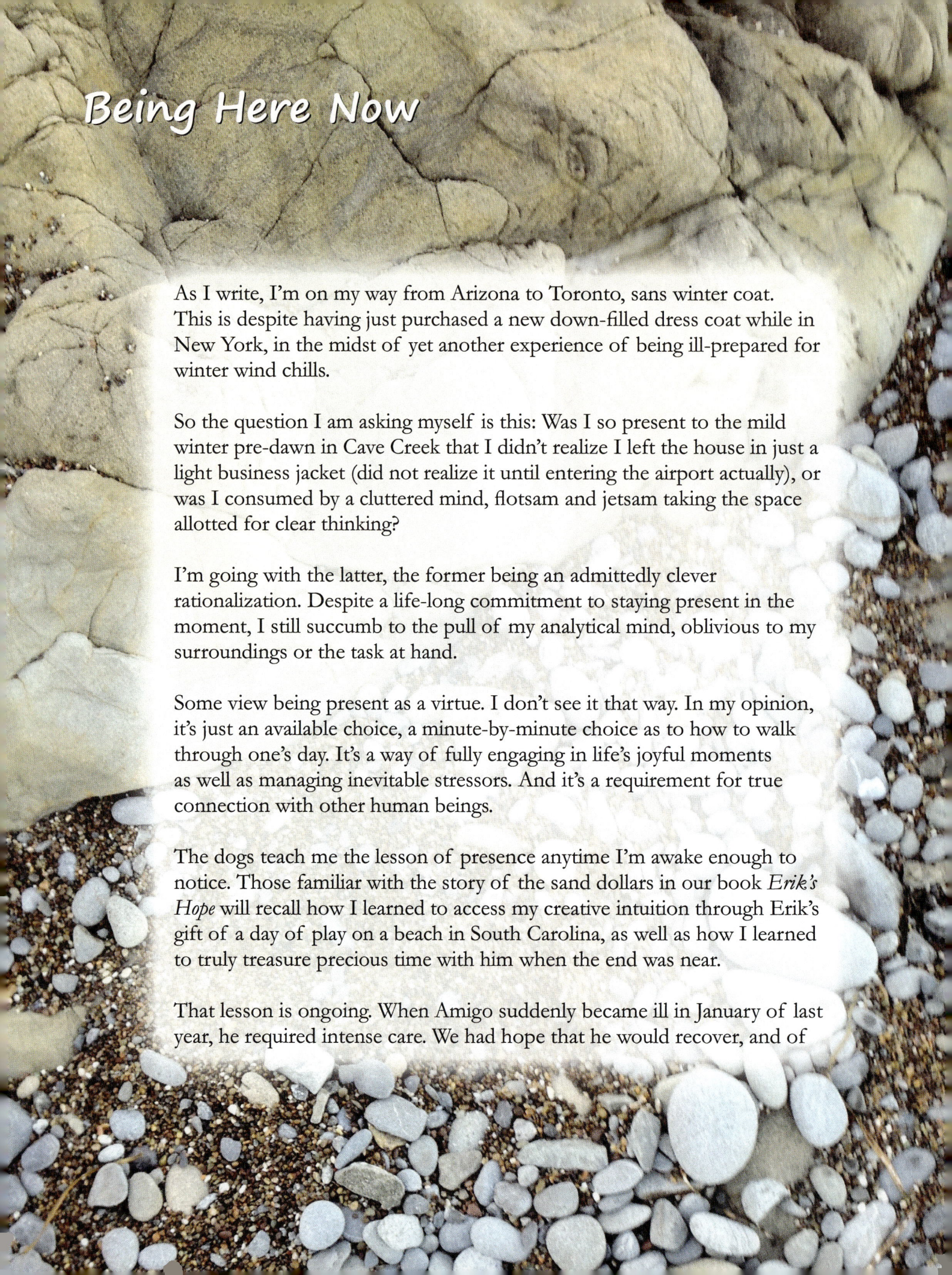

Being Here Now

As I write, I'm on my way from Arizona to Toronto, sans winter coat. This is despite having just purchased a new down-filled dress coat while in New York, in the midst of yet another experience of being ill-prepared for winter wind chills.

So the question I am asking myself is this: Was I so present to the mild winter pre-dawn in Cave Creek that I didn't realize I left the house in just a light business jacket (did not realize it until entering the airport actually), or was I consumed by a cluttered mind, flotsam and jetsam taking the space allotted for clear thinking?

I'm going with the latter, the former being an admittedly clever rationalization. Despite a life-long commitment to staying present in the moment, I still succumb to the pull of my analytical mind, oblivious to my surroundings or the task at hand.

Some view being present as a virtue. I don't see it that way. In my opinion, it's just an available choice, a minute-by-minute choice as to how to walk through one's day. It's a way of fully engaging in life's joyful moments as well as managing inevitable stressors. And it's a requirement for true connection with other human beings.

The dogs teach me the lesson of presence anytime I'm awake enough to notice. Those familiar with the story of the sand dollars in our book *Erik's Hope* will recall how I learned to access my creative intuition through Erik's gift of a day of play on a beach in South Carolina, as well as how I learned to truly treasure precious time with him when the end was near.

That lesson is ongoing. When Amigo suddenly became ill in January of last year, he required intense care. We had hope that he would recover, and of course I wanted to be with him; offering the kind of care only a mother could give. I have a vivid memory of sitting on my bathroom floor as dear Dr. Kit tended to him shortly after surgery. We began to talk of my travel schedule that week, and what I would do. I stopped mid-sentence and said: "I cannot worry about Wednesday, or even tomorrow. I can only manage right now, and now, today, I am here, available and present." That philosophy carried me for three months as Amigo rallied and regressed until his inevitable death. People came along to help when needed and things got done, as they always do. I look back on times like this in my life (and there have been a few this year) and wonder where my stamina came from. I am certain that I channeled my energy wisely, allowing only the matter at hand to *matter*.

The mind is a useful yet tricky tool. Our capacity for conceptualizing, analyzing and calculating is unrivaled in the animal kingdom, and this ability easily seduces our attention away from the matter at hand. It can craft fears and contingencies, and infer meaning that does not exist. Or it can be a brilliant partner to the creative process. Working in tandem, it's as if our heart says, "Here's what I want and need," and our mind says, "Okay, let's figure out how to get that for you."

This summer, a wise friend met my new pup, Kairos. She said, "Andrea, Kairos has an important purpose in your life. He is here to help you tame your 'eagle mind,' and remind you to lead with your heart." One need only look into the depths of his blue eyes to understand that is true.

Yes, I am willing to allow my heart to take the lead. And perhaps I'll remember my coat on my next trip to a chilly city.

Who or what reminds you to **stay present,** to **show up** for what life "presents?"

Reflections on Being Here Now

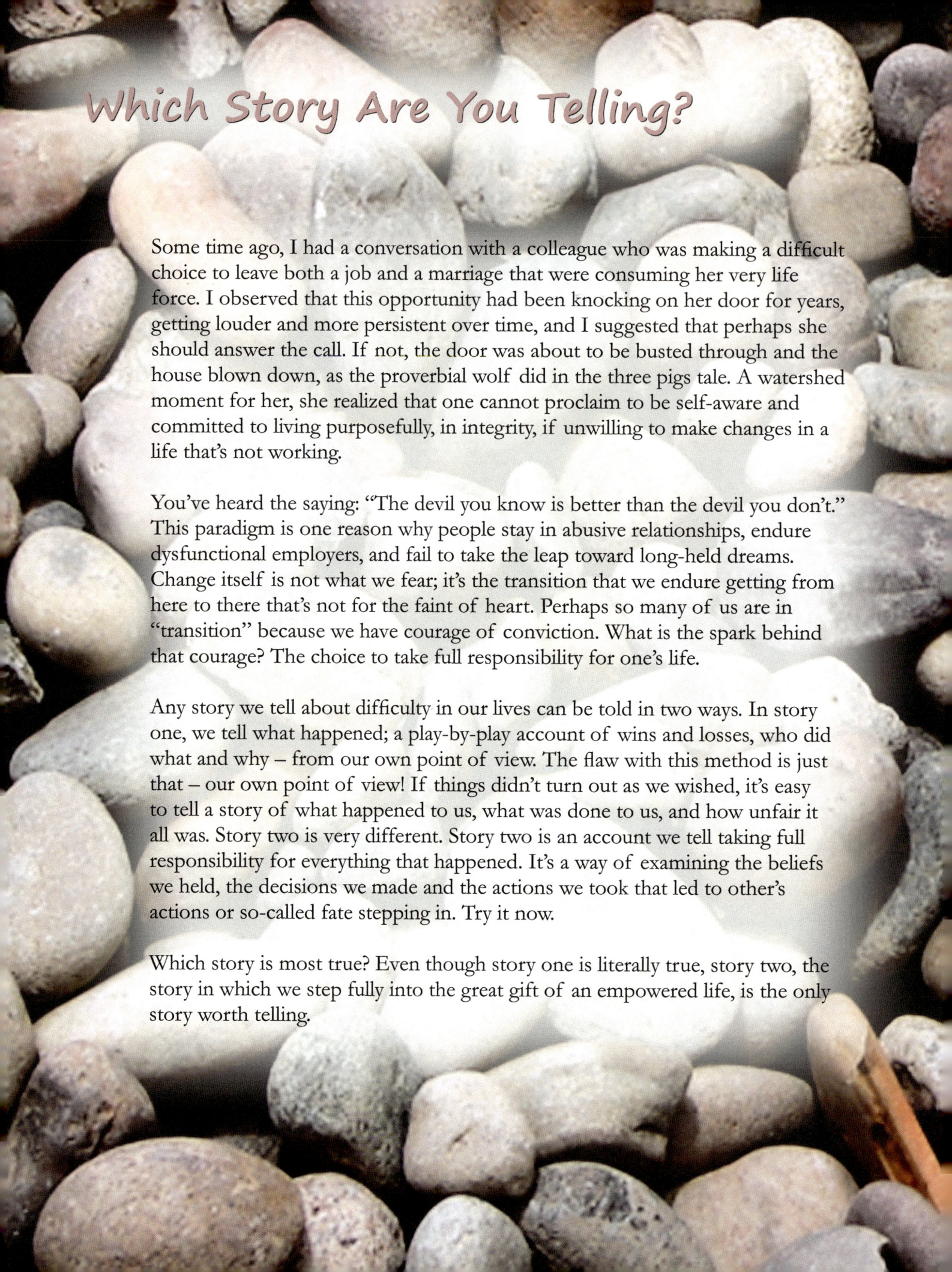

Which Story Are You Telling?

Some time ago, I had a conversation with a colleague who was making a difficult choice to leave both a job and a marriage that were consuming her very life force. I observed that this opportunity had been knocking on her door for years, getting louder and more persistent over time, and I suggested that perhaps she should answer the call. If not, the door was about to be busted through and the house blown down, as the proverbial wolf did in the three pigs tale. A watershed moment for her, she realized that one cannot proclaim to be self-aware and committed to living purposefully, in integrity, if unwilling to make changes in a life that's not working.

You've heard the saying: "The devil you know is better than the devil you don't." This paradigm is one reason why people stay in abusive relationships, endure dysfunctional employers, and fail to take the leap toward long-held dreams. Change itself is not what we fear; it's the transition that we endure getting from here to there that's not for the faint of heart. Perhaps so many of us are in "transition" because we have courage of conviction. What is the spark behind that courage? The choice to take full responsibility for one's life.

Any story we tell about difficulty in our lives can be told in two ways. In story one, we tell what happened; a play-by-play account of wins and losses, who did what and why – from our own point of view. The flaw with this method is just that – our own point of view! If things didn't turn out as we wished, it's easy to tell a story of what happened to us, what was done to us, and how unfair it all was. Story two is very different. Story two is an account we tell taking full responsibility for everything that happened. It's a way of examining the beliefs we held, the decisions we made and the actions we took that led to other's actions or so-called fate stepping in. Try it now.

Which story is most true? Even though story one is literally true, story two, the story in which we step fully into the great gift of an empowered life, is the only story worth telling.

The purpose of story two is never, ever to create guilt or self-blame. Story two's true purpose is to free us to remember we are the causal force in our lives, and our choices and decisions produce our results. Sometimes life does just happen, with serious or tragic consequences. Story two gives us a chance to think or behave in a new way even after a very difficult experience. A liberating idea, don't you think?

My colleague is now living in story two, free from the burden of relinquishing control to others. Easy it is not, and she's befriending the wolf who knocked, learning each day to savor the journey, one step at a time.

If you have recently taken a leap, or if the wolf is at your door and you find yourself considering transition, use story two to create a map, lay out next steps, start anew.

You're in charge of your life.

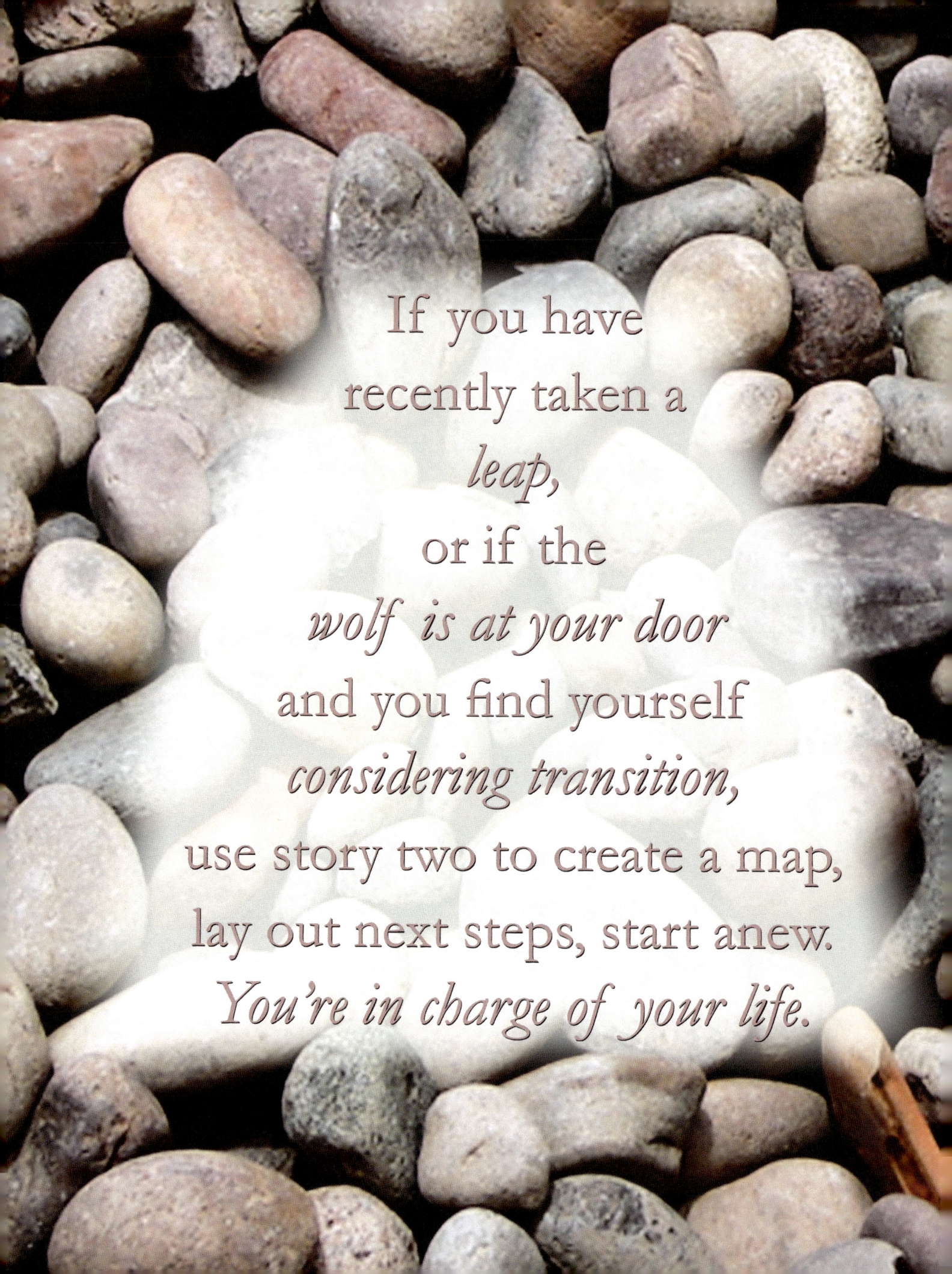

If you have
recently taken a
leap,
or if the
wolf is at your door
and you find yourself
considering transition,
use story two to create a map,
lay out next steps, start anew.
You're in charge of your life.

Reflections on the Story You Are Telling Yourself

"Every transition begins with an ending. We have to let go of
the old thing before we can pick up the new one."
—William Bridges, *Transitions: Making Sense of Life's Changes*

What Is Your Anchor?

So many people are making their way through difficulty, living through turbulence without an anchor. And an anchor can be an important tool for managing the natural fears that arise when life throws surprises at every turn. It's one thing to feel fear and work through it. It's quite another to let fear spiral out of control.

Several years ago, during a trying period of my life, I had a dream that made a profound impact then and became my anchor during future challenges.

In this dream, I found myself driving my car down a steep but very wide paved road. The road was covered with a thick layer of ice and I was having difficulty braking. My car swerved side to side at first, and then began to slide downward, out of control. About the time I realized I could not stop the forward motion, I noticed that the road ended just ahead, the pavement simply cut off and hung over an abyss. It was a look similar to that of a bridge or freeway ramp mid-construction. Just as the front wheels of my car neared the edge, a very large hand arose from the abyss, reached out and stopped my car. Just in the nick of time.

As if this was not enough, I then found myself once again driving on iced pavement, this time in a crowded parking lot. I was driving up and down the aisles, trying to get to the exit and onto the street. I was struggling to maneuver the lanes without hitting parked cars. After several minutes of white-knuckled navigation, I managed to safely exit unharmed, without damaging another vehicle.

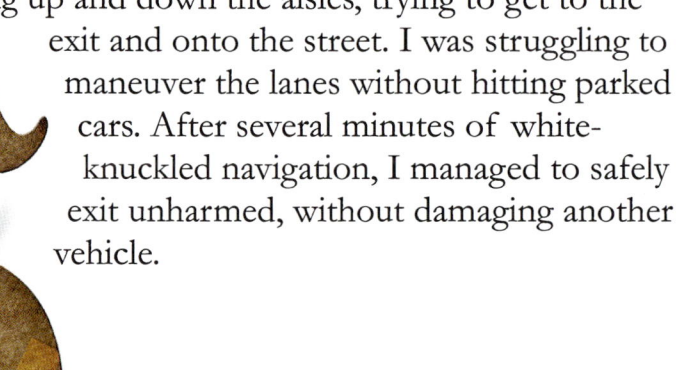

The morning after that dream, I relayed it to a wise friend. Her reply was a question. "Andrea, will you ever again doubt that you are protected?" I hesitated at first, then answered firmly. "No. I have faith that I am indeed safe," I replied.

In the years since, that dream, that *hand,* has served as a reminder that no matter how challenging things become, help is always available – physically or spiritually. The anchor is a comfort to me, as I experience natural and unavoidable fears that accompany a full life.

What is your metaphorical anchor? What do you or can you call upon to remind yourself that even amidst distress, life is still sweet and forgiving, endless possibilities exist, and all will work out?

What is your metaphorical
anchor?

What do you or can you call upon to
remind yourself

that even amidst distress, life is

still sweet and forgiving,

endless possibilities exist
and all will work out?

Reflections on *Faith*

The Year of Your Heart's Desire

Did you make a New Year's resolution this year? If so, stop right now and notice how it *feels*.

Did you sigh wistfully, thinking "the party's over soon," or sense a need to buck up and get discipline? Did the feeling energize you – or deflate you? It's estimated that only 10% of New Year's resolutions are achieved. And it's no wonder, given that they are often uninspired.

The Latin root of the word *resolution* is *resolutionem* – the process of reducing things into simpler forms, loosening or "unbinding." In his *Word Power* blog, Gregory Rineberg points out that in the last 500 or so years, we have used the word *resolution* to mean just the opposite – holding firm in determination, resolute in pursuing a course of action.

Perhaps we can take a lesson from etymology. Consider as a metaphor the loosening or unbinding of your passions and true desires before taking resolved action. I often speak of how intuition can work in tandem with our clever mind to manifest success if we allow our heart to take the lead. "Here is what I want and need," we say from the higher self, our creative center, and then the mind responds, "Okay, let's figure out how to get that for you – here's the right action step to take."

When we lead with our head vs. our heart, we pursue faux goals. A faux goal is a pursuit disguised as noble, but does not truly reflect our heart's desire. Many New Year's resolutions fall into this category. Of course, it sounds honorable to start exercising, get organized or save money… but what's the real reason for taking these actions? Ask yourself these questions:

- Does my goal or resolution reflect a "should" – something I think or have been told I should do?
- Is the goal more important to someone else than it is to me?
- Does the thought of doing or achieving it give me energy or take the wind out of my sails?
- Have I pursued this before without lasting success?

Sometimes we formulate resolutions as some sort of punishment for our supposed failures ("I ate too many holiday desserts" or "I took too much time off"). A goal born out of regret is handicapped from the start.

Examine your goals. What higher purpose is achieved when you get what you say you want? Is *that* your true heart's desire?

Recently, I met a man who was preparing for a second heart bypass surgery. He was disciplined enough to exercise regularly and eat a heart-healthy diet, yet 15 years after the first surgery, he had to endure it again. I asked him where he got the courage and resolve. His reply, "I have five grandchildren and I want to be here as they grow up."

Take inspired action. Lead from your heart. Decide first what you desire, what purpose you are pursuing, then, and only then, define the action steps. Test the actions with the question, "What will that get me?" and include positive effects as well as negative ones – before resolving to achieve them. A helpful hint regarding purposeful action: you'll know it when you feel it, not when you think it.

Our book, *Erik's Hope,* is the culmination of my 13-year pursuit to share the lessons of a shelter dog named Erik with the rest of the world. Once the goal of publication was achieved the journey just began. I have never been filled with more resolve to have this story reach others who can consider and apply the lessons in ways that transform their own lives. My resolve is born out of my deep knowledge that this experience with Erik, this message of hope and inspiration, is purpose-based. It's one of the things I'm here to do in this life, my purpose, and it gives me joy.

So go ahead, resolve to lose weight, save for retirement or leave work earlier. These are noble pursuits for sure. But first ask yourself the question, "What will that get me?" If the answer fills you with passion, if you feel a sense of purpose or meaning, you're on the road to success.

This life we are leading here on planet Earth is finite. While it's fleeting by eternal standards, we all are here now for a reason. Make this the year of your heart's desire.

This life we are
leading here on
planet Earth is
finite.
While it's
fleeting
by eternal standards,
we all are here
now
for a reason.

Make *this* the year of
your heart's desire.

Reflections on Your Heart's Desire

Love In The Midst Of Loss

Today as I awoke, I was struck by the quickening occurring in my life and the lives of those around me. I am in awe of the physical, emotional and spiritual resilience we are demonstrating in the face of challenges and change.

My dear friend, Amigo, left the earth on April 27, 2011. Sweet Kairos showed up in my life just two weeks later on May 12, and arrived home at Morningstar six weeks after that. In the weeks since then, many have asked me, "How can you love a puppy so soon after Amigo's passing?"

My answer is the same each time I'm asked. Loving Kairos does not diminish my grief for the loss of Amigo. I have the capacity to love in the midst of loss, maintain faith in moments of fear, and laugh while I cry. All of us have this capacity and it's being strengthened by the roller coaster experience of life today.

Since Amigo's departure and Kairos' arrival, my husband miraculously survived emergency heart bypass surgery and our book, *Erik's Hope,* was released. Asked many times how I was feeling, my answers included anxiety and anger as well as relief and exhilaration. What has prevailed? Faith, love and gratitude.

In midst of any suffering, there is joy to be found in our lives. I am not referring to the metaphorical "silver lining" that accompanies what appear to be negative experiences. Oh, silver linings indeed exist, though they usually show themselves much later, a result of mental perspective rather than emotional experience. Kairos' arrival was not a silver lining in Amigo's death. Rather, it was a rich reminder of the range of experiences available when we stop, look, listen – and feel. When we open our eyes and hearts fully, we can access all that our lives contain, present and potential.

On Thanksgiving Day, we ceremoniously retired Amigo's harness and spread a portion of his ashes in a remote area of our beloved Cave Creek. Twice, when

I was overcome by the emotion of remembering Amigo's love for that spot and longed to have him there with me, Kairos acted the clown and provided comic relief.

Kairos, like many children, puts everything he sees into his mouth. Fortunately not all is swallowed, but most is at least tasted. As I was digging a hole to bury Amigo's harness in sand and rocks, Kairos buried his face in the sand. He emerged, his white face masked with black granules, with a prized weed hanging from both sides of his mouth. "Look Mom," his innocent and earnest eyes said. "I can help you find what you're looking for. Was it this?"

I was reminded in that moment that one can experience gut-wrenching loss, take in the heady beauty of a pristine natural setting, accept the warm love of a friend, and laugh out loud at the antics of an innocent young dog. All at once, each contributed to the experience of the precious present moment and none was more important than the other.

Erik's Hope chronicles my awakening to simple feelings; feelings that had been buried deep in the sand of my consciousness. It took raw grief to jolt me alive again. I feel truly alive today as I draw upon my own creative intuition to guide me through the rapids. We are being bombarded by experiences and the lesson appears to be, simply, to experience them. Life vests on, enjoy the ride!

Is there a feeling you're keeping hidden away because it's overshadowed by another?

Consider that *you have the capacity* to experience the full range of whatever life serves up.

Reflections on Allowing the Experience at Hand

Mirror Mirror

What if many of the things we hear, see and experience, outside of ourselves, are just reflections of our own inner state? In each of our lives there exist other people and situations acting as mirrors for the aspects of ourselves that we either dislike or admire. If you believe, as I do, that all living things are part of a mass consciousness, separate in personality and possessing free will but connected energetically – spiritually in fact, then this "mirror" principle makes sense. And, as is the case with many of my life lessons, a dog is teaching me just how closely connected we all are.

This past year, I learned that I have a four-legged mirror living in our home, sharing my life. Her name is Whisper. She's a Malamute – my husband's Malamute to be precise, and she's been our companion for eight years. I can hear her comment now, if only she could read. "Yes, it's taken Andrea eight years to get the message. Pitiful humans!"

The truth is, I've always been aware that Whisper reflects my feelings and fears. Whisper shows her sweet and loving demeanor to every human she meets. Other dogs? Not so much. So when we hike in the desert and inevitably run into other dogs, she often takes an aggressive stance, testing my physical strength (a Malamute is a strong creature) and frustrating me as a supposed leader. It would be easy to write her off as impossibly dog-aggressive or rationalize her behavior as protective of me or her handler, but there's more at play here. Whisper mirrors my feelings. If I can remain present, calm and objective, there is usually no trouble. If I feel the fear of a potential fight, or, as is more likely the case, judgment of people who can't or won't control their own dogs, Whisper acts out my emotions.

Knowing this, the solution seems simple – yet managing feelings is far from easy. Dog Whisperer, Cesar Millan, advocates calling up a calm-assertive state of being, using an inside-out approach of managing one's thoughts and feelings before taking outward action. I challenge you to try it now.

Imagine some person or group for whom you

feel judgment – from mild superiority to true disdain or contempt – the degree does not matter. We all have these feelings at times. Okay, now that you've got it, try to release it. Stop feeling judgment, quickly. Tough, yes? For me, it can be very difficult and at the same time, a very worthwhile pursuit. If I can manage my thoughts and feelings, then I can manage my actions – and this, in my opinion, is the key to the universe.

Go back to the judgmental state you just identified. What is this person or situation reflecting that is true for you? Do you feel a fear that was previously unrecognized? Is there some aspect of the other person's behavior that triggers a memory of your own shortcomings, a mistake you made, a lesson you learned? Identify it, feel it, and – here's the magic – it will be transformed.

Once a previously unconscious emotion is brought to the surface, your logical mind can make sense of it, and you can act appropriately. Take the feeling of fear, for example. If the fear represents a real threat, you can act on that. If the fear is based on history or a habit of thought, you can let it go. The truth will indeed set us free.

There's a bonus to this process, given that we are all connected. When we transform our inner state, others respond in new ways. It makes for a more peaceful hike, as well as a better world.

We are all connected. When we transform our inner state, others respond in new ways.

Reflections on the Mirrors in Your Life

It's How You Play the Game

On a lark, I entered an amateur photo contest. Howling Dog Alaska's shout out for fun pics of dogs wearing their awesome gear. To my surprise, my photo was chosen as a top 15 finalist. The winners were to be selected through online voting. "Okay," I thought, "this might be fun." I posted the link on my Facebook page and emailed a few friends asking them to vote for my shot. I was only mildly engaged and soon it was off my mind.

Until my husband, Arthur, got involved.

Arthur is a retired sales executive and race car driver. I tend to forget about his competitive nature, as it's not something that shows up in our day-to-day relationship. Competition has a place, and our marriage is not one of those places. So in telling Arthur about the contest, I didn't realize I had unleashed a force.

He went to work immediately, calling and emailing friends, asking them to vote. So far so good. Then I learned he was asking my friends (who love him and smiled when sharing this) to ask their friends and family members to vote. This was a little over the top in my opinion, but no harm done.

As days went on, three top contenders emerged. My photo was one of them. Arthur became relentless, checking standings and appealing to mere acquaintances for votes.

Puzzled and a little concerned, I asked him why this contest was so important to him. With a huge grin, he replied, "Because I like to win."

To win means to succeed or triumph – a constructive thing for sure. Yet, in my life and in my work, I have seen misplaced competition destroy relationships, teams and businesses. There's a team exercise I lead in which the object is to work together to achieve an outcome. Almost without exception, members of the group work against one another, competing vs. collaborating with other team members. In doing so, they inevitably lose the game.

Winning and competitiveness are highly misunderstood. Even the dictionary's definition of "competitive" seems pejorative: "Inclined toward wanting to achieve more than others." Competition's synonyms include words such as "rivalry," "opposition" and "war." Ugh.

I view real competitiveness, the kind that my husband demonstrates, as a drive to win – not a drive to destroy someone or something else. I asked him what he gets out of winning – what it does for his psyche, if you will. He told me he gets a tremendous amount of satisfaction knowing he has done all he can, knowing he's done his best.

Yesterday, as the race heated up and the end drew near, I decided to test that. I said to Arthur, "Let's suppose one of the other contenders owns a small business, of, say 50 employees. And let's pretend that on the last day of the contest, she asks all her employees to vote, rendering you out of the running. What then?"

His reply, "If that scenario actually happens, then I'll be satisfied because I've done my best. It's not about what the others do, Andrea, it's about what I do."

I was reminded of the famous (and controversial) saying attributed to sportswriter Grantland Rice: "It's not whether you win or lose, it's how you play the game."

How do you "play the game" of life? Do you view competition and winning as a negative thing – and in so doing, give away your power to succeed? Or do you compete for the sake of it, using up your resources in an effort to win at any cost? Take a lesson from the photo contest. Challenge the notion that if there's a winner, there must be a loser.

29

How do you "play the game" of life?

Do you view competition and winning as a negative thing — and in so doing, give away your power to succeed?

Or do you compete for the sake of it, using up your resources in an effort to win at any cost?

Take a lesson from the photo contest. Challenge the notion that if there's a winner, there must be a loser.

Reflections on How You Play the Game

A Week Full of Grace

It's a joy to share my experiences by writing a weekly blog, in the hopes that readers will relate to something I have to say, or take away a tool that makes their path a little smoother. Because we're all connected, rarely does one of us have an experience that is not shared by many more.

When I embark on that creative process, I look back at the week before. This time, I notice that for the first time in a long time, the week was uneventful in the dramatic sense, and did not present its usual overflowing suitcase of lessons. For this, I am grateful. As I review each day, my gratitude deepens.

In their book, *Character Strengths and Virtues*, Chris Peterson and Martin Seligman refer to gratitude's Latin root, the word "gratia" or "grace" and define it as "kindness, generousness, gifts, the beauty of giving and receiving, or getting something for nothing." Grace. Yes, a week full of grace.

As I begin to list the things I am thankful for, some seem small, while others are more high-impact and far-reaching. Yet, as I consider the energy of "grace," it knows no limits or boundaries. Grace is, for me, a feeling, and it sets forth an entire chain of positive events no one can predict or measure. As like attracts like, it grows.

I am grateful for, first and foremost, the relationships in my life. Last week's work was ordinary. The people I worked with made it extraordinary. I am grateful for trusting bonds with old clients and the willingness for new ones to take risks in order to grow.

Life outside work, with my husband and my friends, was sweet and simple. I appreciate supermarket flowers when I had a headache, hiking buddies and humor. And of course, I am grateful for the unconditional love of the dogs.

The list could go on. I was even graced by two potentially difficult but flawless connecting flights, finalist status in a meaningless (but quite fun) photo contest, and the time to get everything done, for once. I feel like a very lucky girl.

I like this energy, this grace, so I think I'll linger here for awhile … maybe for the entire week.

Care to join me? There's space for everyone.

"Every day offers us simple gifts when we are willing to search our hearts for the place that's right for each of us."
– Sarah Ban Breathnach, *Simple Abundance: A Daybook of Comfort and Joy*

I like this energy, this grace, so I think I'll linger here for awhile … maybe for the entire week.

*Care to join me?
There's space for everyone.*

Reflections on Gratitude

My Left Leg

I've always been pretty good at logic and analysis, calculating and thinking. Having just begun feeling in earnest late into my 30's, I am still somewhat new to it. (Yes, that's a bit of a joke as all of us feel – yet it is new for me to give credence to my more intuitive and creative side). And just when I think I have the right brain-left brain, head-heart thing in balance, whammo – I get hit with a lesson – a lesson that involves the mind-body connection.

For the past four years I've been studying and practicing (but not yet mastering), a form of Pilates that has virtually changed my life. The discipline, an invention of the talented Dana Sterling of Carefree Movement, has eliminated back pain and frequent headaches, and has built strength I never knew was possible. A good example of the principle "simple not easy," it's not a mere workout routine but rather a new way to sit, stand, sleep and breathe, 24-7. Who knew it would impact how I think and interact with others?

Among other things during these focused four years, I have been striving to balance my weight on both sides of my body, rather than using only my right side for strength, straining and stretching my left mercilessly. My posture has improved vastly, and my leg strength is – well, more or less is – balanced. So what a surprise when a Chi Gong instructor, someone I regard as a masterful, intuitive teacher remarked to me, "Andrea, you walk with your weight on your right side only, barely skimming the surface with your left foot. What are you holding back from yourself and the world?"

He went on to explain how my lack of left side physical connection to the earth could be restricting my connection to my right brain, that feeling-based center that I have come to realize is the driver of everything. Damn, damn, damn. I thought I was doing so well.

The fact is, I was doing well to that point. But there's so much more. Perhaps I'm still allowing my logical know-it-all left hemisphere to be in charge, by default.

So why am I sharing this story with you here? It seems to present a reinforcement of an often-pondered principle. Your right brain represents the creative force. It signifies perfection not yet manifest. Your left brain is the doing force, the active, willing servant. In perfect balance, creative intuition says: "Here is what I want and need. Here is the life I choose to live and the types of people and experiences that make it fulfilling." The logical, efficient analytic side says: "You want that? I'll get it for you. Here's what we need to do…"

As I was writing this piece, my friend shared a lesson from her golf coach. She's learning to use her whole body in her swing, rather than default to her dominant side. The outcome? She no longer hesitates over the ball, analyzing to the point of destroying her presence.

I don't know if you rely on the right side of your body to drag the rest of you around as you go about your busy days (though it's actually a very common pattern). But if you are allowing past messages and memories, or so-called logic to usurp your creative knowing in any area of your life, notice how you're standing.

Which way are you leaning?

Reflections on Balance

What I Control

I was talking with a friend who, like me, turned fifty this year. After a lighthearted lament about physical aging, we shared one treasured outcome of this age: the settled-in quality that comes from knowing ourselves so well. We both agreed that regarding our many personality traits, good and bad, knowing and accepting ourselves is the most important thing.

Understanding what sparks our spirit, as well as what pushes our buttons, gives us the ultimate freedom, the ultimate control. We can choose to limit our experiences to those we prefer, or we can manage our reaction to those things (usually provoked by other people) that cause stress. Clearly this knowledge and subsequent liberty is not limited to those fifty and over. But it is an interesting phenomenon. At about this age, those who would hide their apparent flaws begin to admit their humanness, and those who would refrain from acknowledging their unique strengths begin to name them, out loud. Finally, because we have conscious awareness, we can control our experience of the world. Can you hear the choir singing "Hallelujah!"?

Toward the end of our conversation, my friend, who errs on the side of humility, declared: "One thing I'm not is controlling!" And thus began an afternoon of self-analysis regarding the issue of self-awareness… and control.

A master of self-control, I've never been one to try to control other people, perhaps because I would abhor the idea that someone would do that to me. But I *have* tried to control the universe, and anyone who knows me well would likely smile at this statement. During this 50th year, I learned that control is a myth.

It is futile.

Perhaps trying to the control the universe – life and death, fate and providence – for fifty years simply makes one weary. Now I smile at the thought that I was ever in control of anything. Except my experience.

In one of my favorite passages from *A New Earth,* Eckhart Tolle speaks of the peace that comes from accepting the circumstances of the present moment, and the suffering that ensues if one's focus is on what could have been or might be. I believe the same can be said of control. When one tries to control that which can't be managed or directed, suffering results. Surrender gives us, paradoxically, the ability to control our reaction. We can choose to accept or resist, endure or avoid, judge or embrace.

My friend and I embrace the many blessings that define our lives, not the least of which are the unique traits – quirks included – that make us who we are. These very traits are what guided our many decisions and created the lives we live. We are happy in an imperfect world, mostly because we know who we are and what we contribute to others in small ways and large.

Is there a quality of your being, a quality uniquely you, that you could take out, brush off and embrace?

Try it for an hour or a day – and notice how comforting the feeling is. Surrender to the truth of it instead of trying to hide, change or control it. Those around you might notice too.

Is there a quality of your being, a quality uniquely you, that you could take out, brush off and embrace?

Try it for an hour or a day – and notice how comforting the feeling is. Surrender to the truth of it instead of trying to hide, change or control it.

Those around you might notice too.

Reflections on Control

Becoming the Change

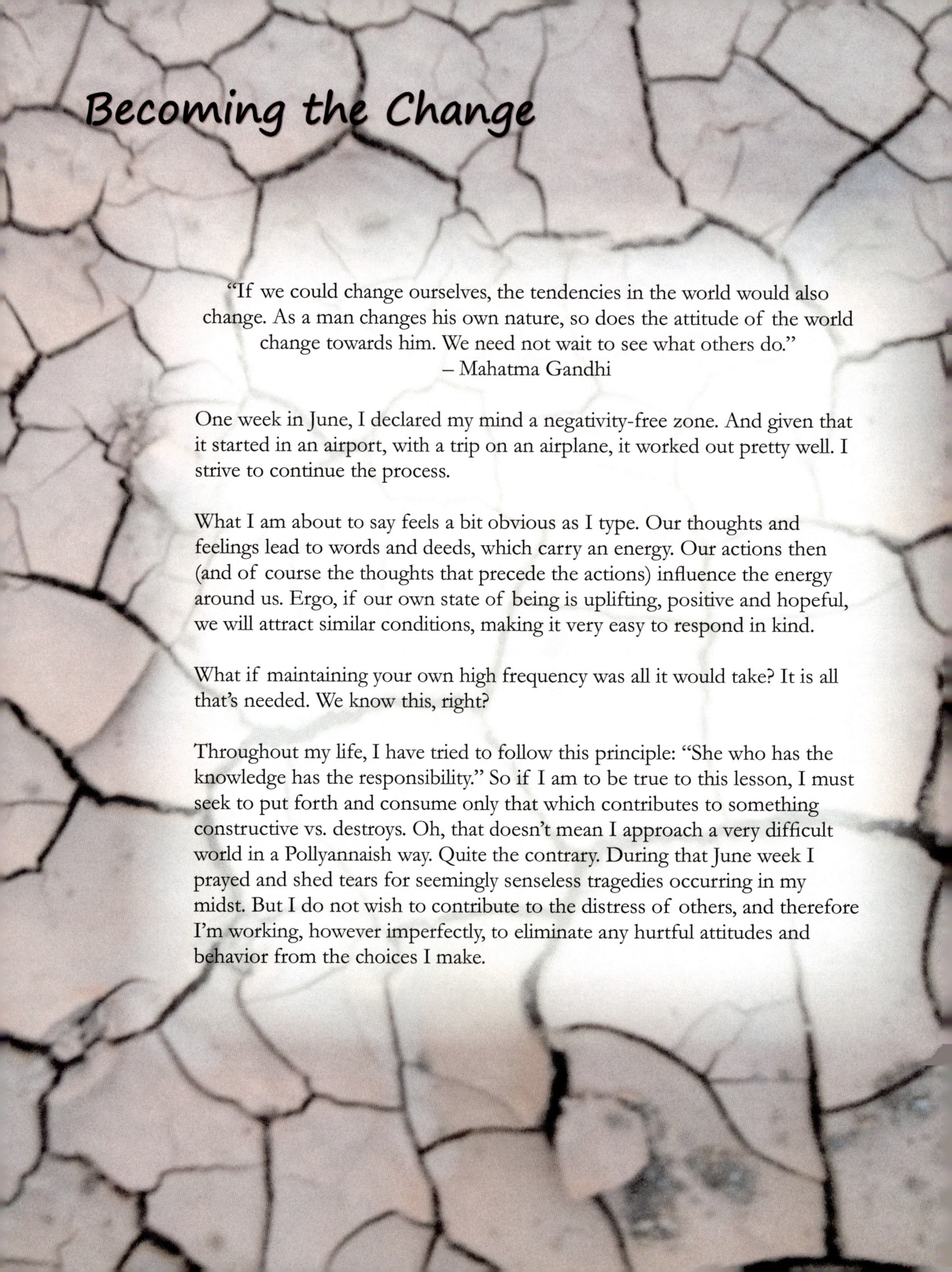

"If we could change ourselves, the tendencies in the world would also change. As a man changes his own nature, so does the attitude of the world change towards him. We need not wait to see what others do."
– Mahatma Gandhi

One week in June, I declared my mind a negativity-free zone. And given that it started in an airport, with a trip on an airplane, it worked out pretty well. I strive to continue the process.

What I am about to say feels a bit obvious as I type. Our thoughts and feelings lead to words and deeds, which carry an energy. Our actions then (and of course the thoughts that precede the actions) influence the energy around us. Ergo, if our own state of being is uplifting, positive and hopeful, we will attract similar conditions, making it very easy to respond in kind.

What if maintaining your own high frequency was all it would take? It is all that's needed. We know this, right?

Throughout my life, I have tried to follow this principle: "She who has the knowledge has the responsibility." So if I am to be true to this lesson, I must seek to put forth and consume only that which contributes to something constructive vs. destroys. Oh, that doesn't mean I approach a very difficult world in a Pollyannaish way. Quite the contrary. During that June week I prayed and shed tears for seemingly senseless tragedies occurring in my midst. But I do not wish to contribute to the distress of others, and therefore I'm working, however imperfectly, to eliminate any hurtful attitudes and behavior from the choices I make.

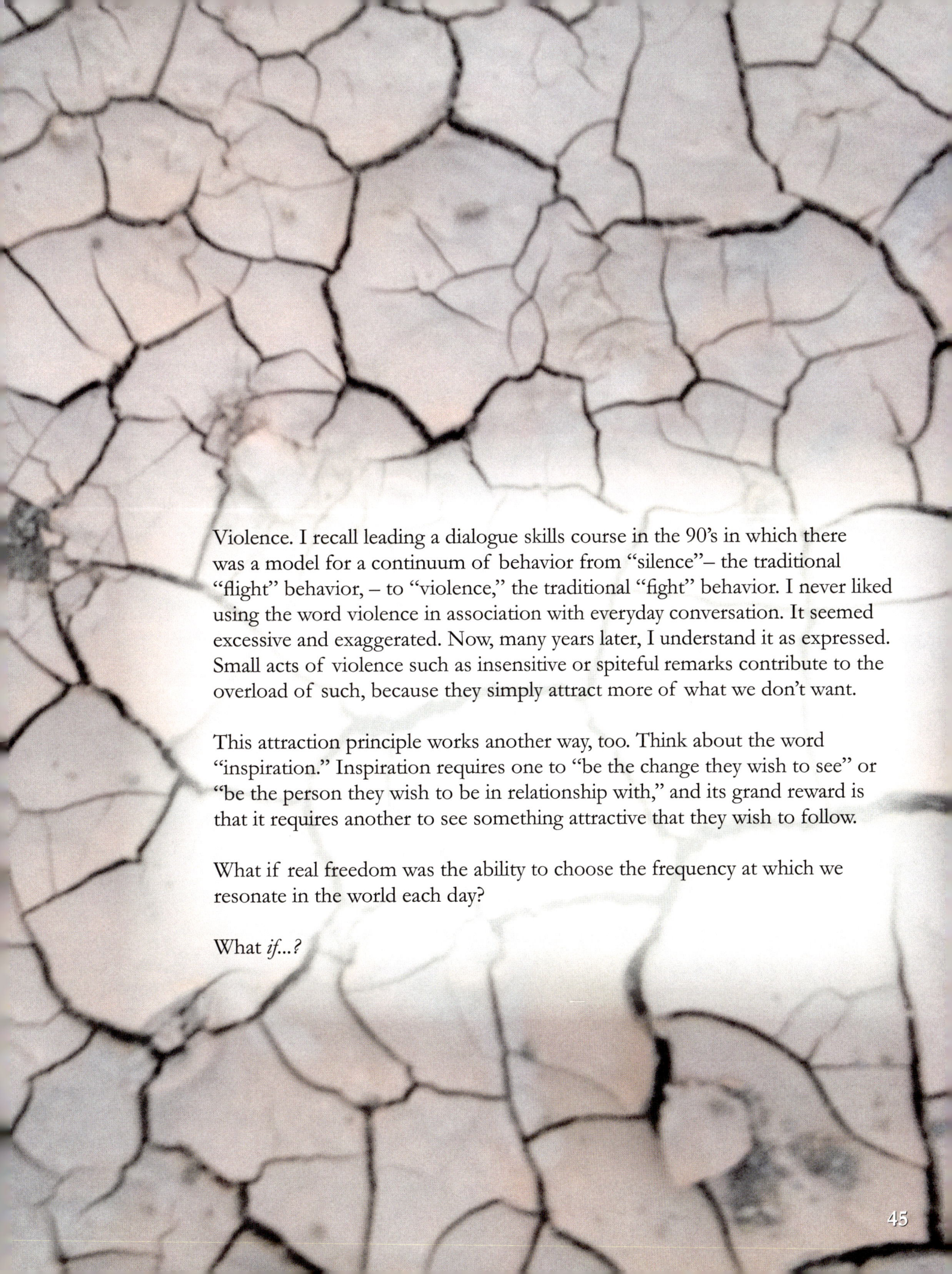

Violence. I recall leading a dialogue skills course in the 90's in which there was a model for a continuum of behavior from "silence"– the traditional "flight" behavior, – to "violence," the traditional "fight" behavior. I never liked using the word violence in association with everyday conversation. It seemed excessive and exaggerated. Now, many years later, I understand it as expressed. Small acts of violence such as insensitive or spiteful remarks contribute to the overload of such, because they simply attract more of what we don't want.

This attraction principle works another way, too. Think about the word "inspiration." Inspiration requires one to "be the change they wish to see" or "be the person they wish to be in relationship with," and its grand reward is that it requires another to see something attractive that they wish to follow.

What if real freedom was the ability to choose the frequency at which we resonate in the world each day?

What *if...?*

What if
real freedom
was the
ability to choose
the frequency at which we resonate
in the world each day?
What *if*...?

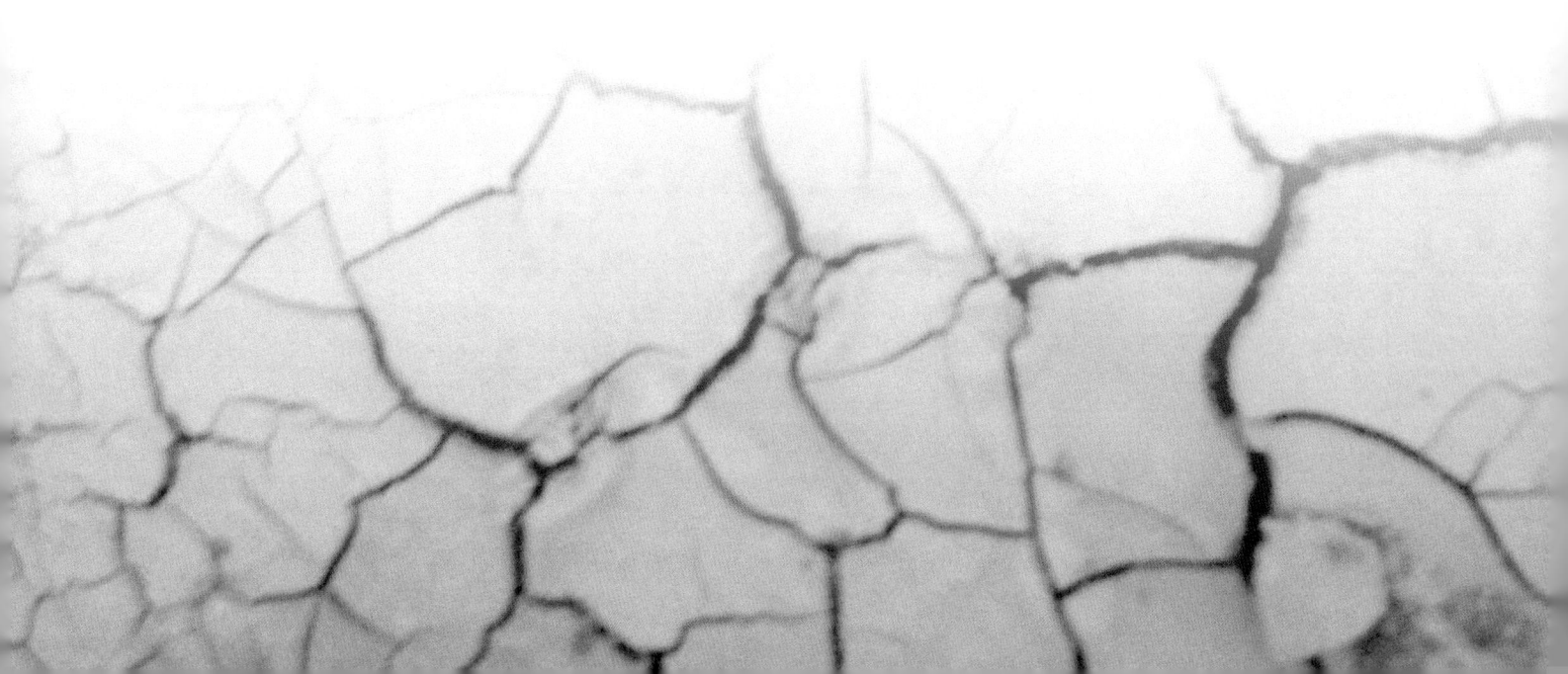

Reflections on Becoming the Change

It Took A Village

What could you accomplish for yourself or for the world if you were to call upon the generosity of friends? Your request just might be the gift they were waiting for.

I am blessed to live in a small community where neighbors help one another. The notion that "it takes a village" to accomplish tasks is often literally true for us. So when I found myself agreeing to temporarily house and re-home a rescued Siberian Husky, I had to call in the villagers.

Young Huskies are a handful, and as a team we were able to care for, feed and exercise this needy one, while arranging for air transportation (no small feat in Arizona's summer heat) to his forever home in North Carolina.

If I were to list out all the things friends and neighbors did to help, it would exceed these pages. We had helpers from the neighborhood as well as from other states. Those closest to the action would say that the whole exercise gave them an opportunity to break from their routines, slow down, get some exercise – and laugh. A perfect way to spend the Memorial Day weekend in my opinion!

The experience made me think about all the give and take that is contained in friendship. It reminded me of the comfortable latitude we have to push up against others' limits, while at the same time being open to an answer of "no." Most of all, it illustrated a simple and powerful but often forgotten principle: when we give, we get.

My lesson in this? If you want or need something done, ask for help! I've written about this before, and probably will continue to learn this lesson until the day I die. Over the years I have relaxed my quid pro quo stance, no longer feeling the need to reciprocate an equal kindness to the precise person showing one to me. Oh, I must balance the scales and certainly give back when I get something for myself, but it's not a one-for-one transaction. I truly believe that what we sow, we reap. Those who help me get a return on their effort, from me or some other source. It's just the way it works.

Next time you ask for help (or even hesitate to do so), remind yourself that you're offering the other person the opportunity to fulfill their own drive for generosity – a true win-win arrangement.

What could you accomplish for yourself or for the world if you were to gather the villagers?

Your request just might be the gift they were waiting for.

What could you accomplish *for yourself* or *for the world* if you were to gather the villagers?

Your request just might be the *gift* they were waiting for.

Reflections on Giving and Getting

I Just Assumed…

As I have written before, others often serve as a mirror for our own behaviors. So when we who possess a degree of self-awareness examine those whom we judge, therein lies opportunity. Lately I've been judging people who make assumptions, so I suppose I had better look in the mirror.

Assumptions. I write about them, teach people how to become aware of them and uncover "the truth" – and I wrestle with my own. I probably will continue to study the fascinating field of assumptions until I can rid my very essence of them on the journey to freedom.

It irritates me when people make assumptions about how I am feeling (there are times I'm not even sure myself), whether I really mean what I just said (most of the time I do, at least in that moment) or my motives (just ask and I'll tell you). Much of this falls into the category of the compassionate: "You must be exhausted!" (no, I'm hungry) or the mundane: "You really don't mind driving?" (I would not have offered if I minded).

Sometimes though, the assumptions we make are far less benign. They are a result of unexamined perspective. Driven by a locked-in, self-referenced point of view, these judgmental perceptions can be damaging to, among other things, the relationships we hold as important. They allow us to make up fantasies of how and why we have been betrayed by another, and they serve to separate us from those with whom we seek the closest connection. At their worst, they inform future actions and decisions based on a false belief system.

No wonder I want to free myself of them!

I consider myself a flexible, broad thinker, most of the time pragmatic, and very open to debate about my opinions and perspectives. Yet I can make self-centered assumptions that then lead to conclusions, which, left unexamined, can dramatically affect the ways in which I interact with others. Dialogue guru Chris Argyris describes this phenomenon with his classic Ladder of Inference. He demonstrates how easy it is to behave based on misinformation (our assumptions vs. the facts), and how to break the cycle.

We climb Argyris' metaphorical ladder the moment we make an observation. First we select the parts of the experience to focus on, then rapidly add meaning, make assumptions and draw conclusions, based on our own past experiences. With repeated selective observations, we solidify our conclusions as belief systems – and then, here's the real danger – we take future action based on our sometimes flawed beliefs. This sets up the classic self-fulfilling prophecy wherein those around us behave pretty much as we expect, however disappointing that behavior may be.

So what to do? First, realize we all make assumptions and jump to conclusions – it's how the human brain works. Then, equipped with this knowledge, clarify. Own your assumptions by using phrases like "I think…" or "My assumption is…," followed by a question to check them out. "How do you see it?" or, "Is that accurate?"

Experience assures me that these gems of wisdom reap huge rewards. Try it today with someone important to you.

I will too.

Our ability to achieve the results we truly desire is eroded by our feelings that:
- Our beliefs are the truth.
- The truth is obvious.
- Our beliefs are based on real data.
- The data we select are the real data.

~ Rick Ross

Reflections on Freedom from Assumptions

Heart-Inspired Action

I'm reflecting on a recent lunch with a dynamic woman who I admire greatly. She owns and manages a thriving business, juggling multiple priorities in work and life. Her secret? The relationships she builds and nurtures.

I'm fascinated by how she makes time to do the things she does to build trusting, sometimes life-long bonds with customers, vendors and employees, (not to mention while caring for an active family and supporting philanthropic interests). She does the small yet high-impact things I think about yet often don't follow through on. She forges personal connections by genuinely acknowledging the trials and triumphs of her colleagues' multi-faceted lives.

Whether it's a piece of welcome information or advice contained in an otherwise mundane email, or a greeting card celebrating a small accomplishment or sharing compassion, my friend takes inspired action. It's inspired because she has true empathy and concern for those her business touches. It's not a technique … it comes from the heart. If you've ever had the urge or feeling to offer comfort or congratulate, but either shied away or gotten too busy, take a lesson from Jane Spicer, of Daphne's Headcovers. She feels the need, then acts. Impeccably.

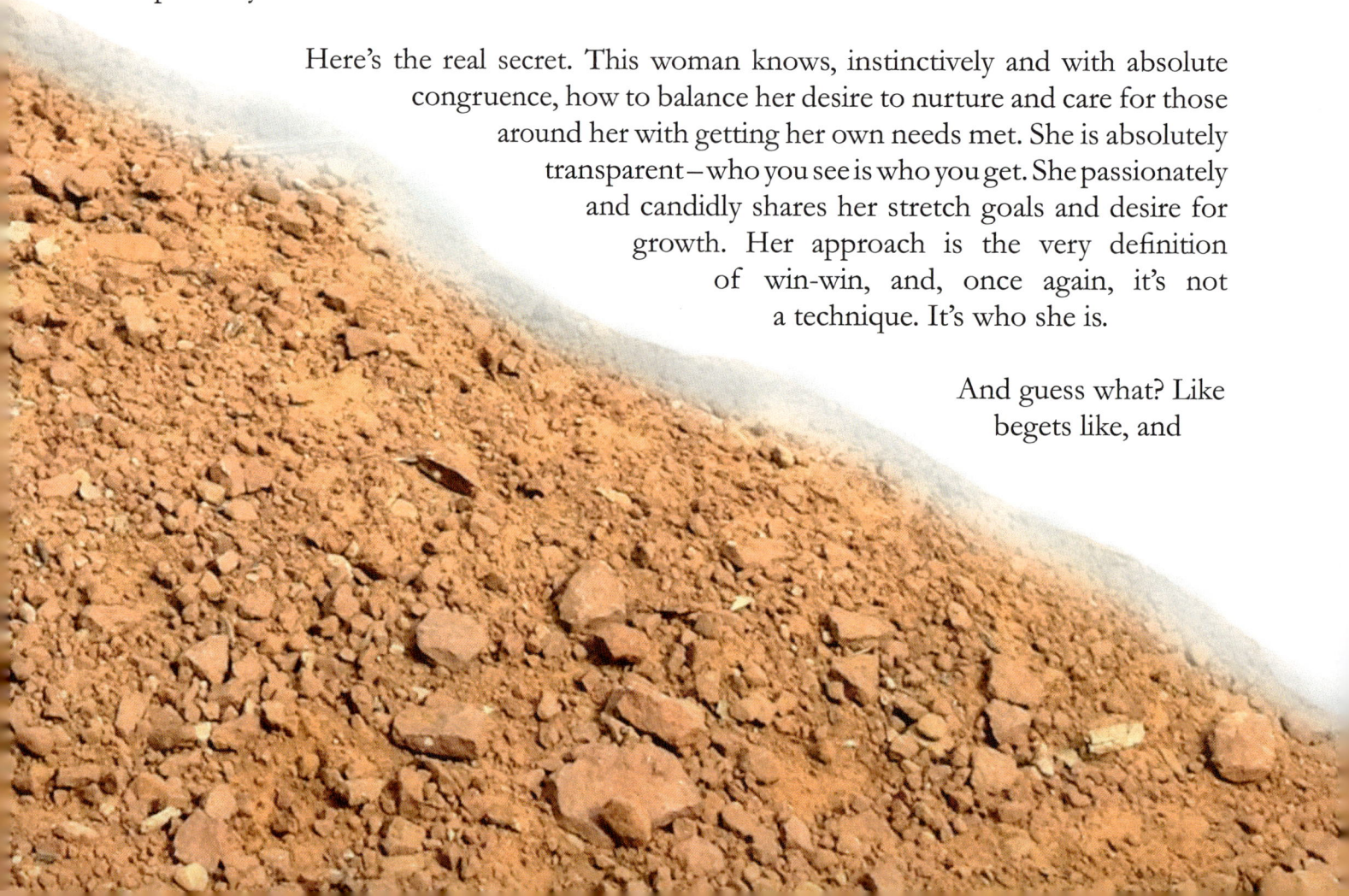

Here's the real secret. This woman knows, instinctively and with absolute congruence, how to balance her desire to nurture and care for those around her with getting her own needs met. She is absolutely transparent—who you see is who you get. She passionately and candidly shares her stretch goals and desire for growth. Her approach is the very definition of win-win, and, once again, it's not a technique. It's who she is.

And guess what? Like begets like, and

others strive to help her. Jane has an army of people committed to her business' mission who aren't on her payroll. And there are smaller benefits too. When the inevitable minor problems of business life occur, the "funds" in the relationship bank serve as a comforting cushion, and no one overreacts.

So many people ask for help, yet have no cushion from which to draw in the relationship bank. Others give without considering their own needs, rendering those needs unmet and success elusive. One without the other is unproductive.

It's no longer a secret. Act from the heart. Share of yourself openly while declaring what you too want and need. You might be surprised at what follows.

It's no longer a secret.
Act from the heart.
Share of yourself *openly*
while declaring what
you too *want* and *need*.
You might be surprised
at what *follows*.

Reflections on Acting on Your Heart's Messages

Still, I Learn

I am in the 24th year of a happy marriage. While that clearly does not make me a marriage expert, friends often study our relationship for clues to success secrets in a world where so many fail for so many different reasons. As they study, I learn.

Most people notice our independence, our personality differences and our apparent love for one another. While I would not suggest the former two are essentials for happy, long-term, intimate relationships as a rule, they are indeed essentials in ours. We share certain core beliefs and values, yet our interests vary. We give one another the freedom and space to pursue diverse interests independent of the other. A good example is that throughout Arthur's entire car racing career, I rarely accompanied him. The simple reason was this: I don't care for the sound or the smell of race car engines. When people ask me, an avid hiker, why Arthur rarely joins me and the dogs on our adventures, I tell the truth: he doesn't like to get his feet dirty.

The secret to our personality differences lies not in the ways in which we are alike or different, but in that we know and are comfortable with ourselves. That's the basic price of admission for relating to another person, especially one you live and share life with.

I've always been curious about others' observations about the third theme, our mutual love. While I get it, I've wondered what other people see. This year, this very difficult 24th year, has provided insight.

I'm going to share something here for the whole world to read. Indulge me please, as it seems like a big revelation: Arthur is 29 years older than I. Always healthy, racing cars and caring for horses, he never showed his age until one day this past October, when he nearly died. Emergency heart surgery saved his life, he recovered and is literally in better shape than before. As is our marriage.

So back to the question, how do people "see" our love? They see our kindness to one another. They see that we tolerate and even appreciate each other's quirks. When I travel, Arthur quietly fills my inevitably (and sometimes purposely) empty gas tank, and I prep and plate his salads so he'll remember to eat them. Oh, we get irritated sometimes, and I'm clearly the one who is less tolerant – but since Arthur's illness, he will rarely engage me in pettiness. I am learning.

Arthur has always had more patience than me, yet now his seems endless. I am learning. When you live with someone who goes about his day as if every minute of life is precious, you can't help but cherish the simple moments in life. Shared comfort in the simple moments, care for one another's well being, and joy in the other's accomplishments define real intimacy for us. And still each day I am learning, as is he.

Our relationship is happy, not perfect. It is kind, yet human. It is flexible, generous and most of all it is uniquely ours. If others can gain insight from observation, we are willing subjects as we continue to grow together.

The secret to our personality differences lies not in the ways in which we are alike or different, but in that we know and are comfortable with ourselves.

Reflections on Learning from Your Relationships

The "Nothing" That is Everything

I never tire of the daily notes I receive from Mike Dooley's brilliant Totally Unique Thoughts (TUT), my personalized subscription to *Notes from the Universe*. But this Monday's message was a jolt: "Remember, you will always have friends, guides, and love, Andrea, but no one is coming to 'save you.' That's the adventure package you signed up for."

The Universe went on to say that the only one who would save me was me, and assured me that I had guaranteed superpowers with which to do so.

Now I have never required "saving," though I have considerable experience wishing, hoping and praying. When I read the message I was reminded of two experiences.

During one particularly challenging time, a dear friend asked, in earnest and with deep compassion, "What can I do?" "Nothing!" I replied too sharply, then I softened. "Just be you," I said. "Be my friend."

Nothing to do, no-thing. The nothing that is everything.

The second is an experience I recount in our book, *Erik's Hope*. Faced with potential tragedy, I prayed. All at once, for the first time ever, I was overcome by a feeling of profound aloneness. In that instant, I realized that prayer is a conversation between the part of us that is God and the part of us that is human. The human part needed to take action. Fueled by sheer life force, the spirit that I am (and that TUT is no doubt referring to), I took inspired action and rallied others to help. In the moment, it felt like no effort at all. No-thing, just flow. It worked out beautifully.

Even with this realization, I still puzzled over TUT's words. Not even love will save me? In my heart, I have always believed John Lennon's mantra, "All you need is love." Then it dawned on me. I am love. You are love. The part of us that's love is the guaranteed superpower. Love is inside, not out. That kind of love is all we need.

Our true power is immense beyond measure. It is a state of being – the nothing that is everything – to give as well as to receive.

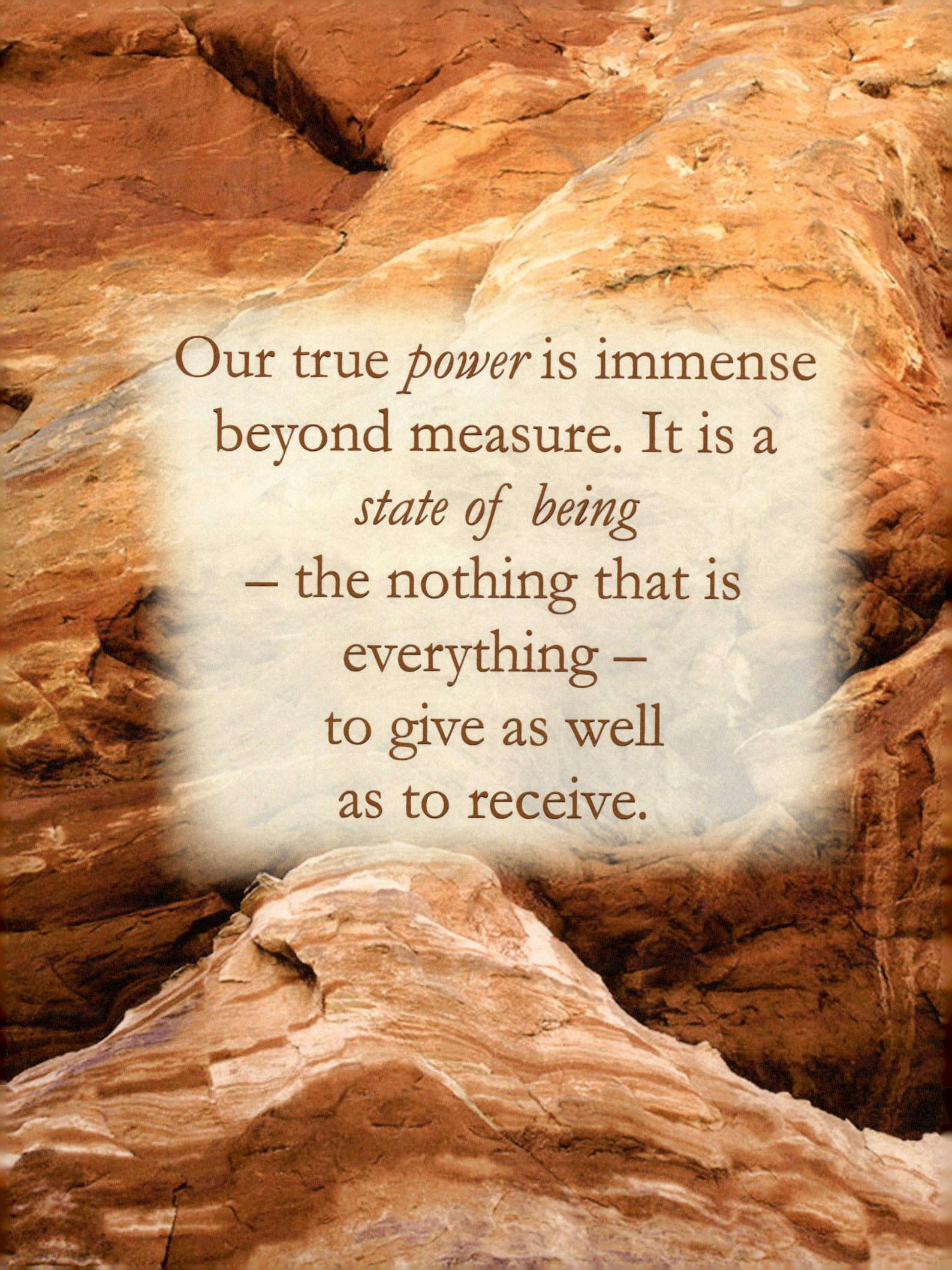

Our true *power* is immense beyond measure. It is a *state of being* — the nothing that is everything — to give as well as to receive.

Reflections on Nothing

A Pack of Friends or One at a Time?

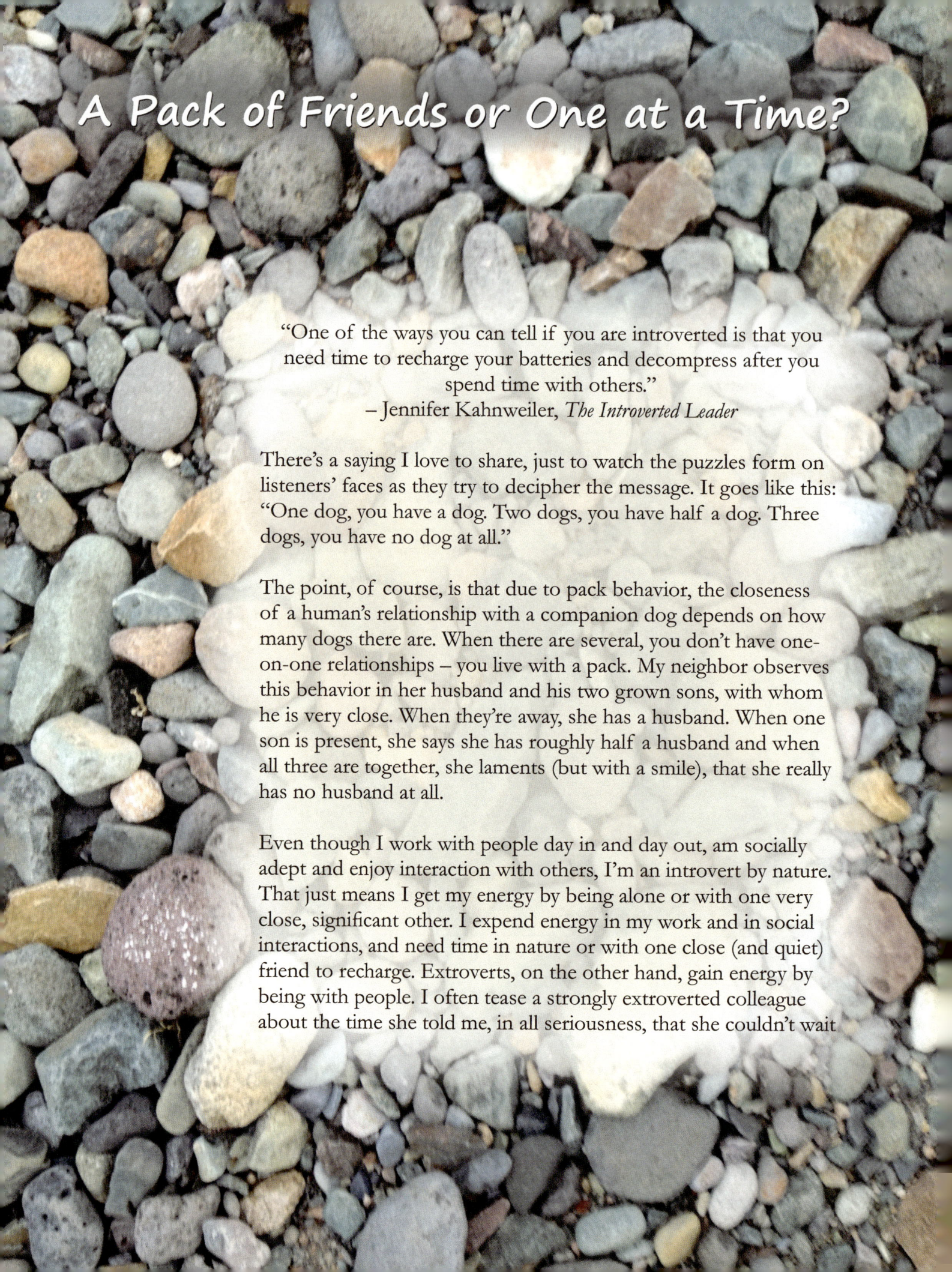

"One of the ways you can tell if you are introverted is that you need time to recharge your batteries and decompress after you spend time with others."
– Jennifer Kahnweiler, *The Introverted Leader*

There's a saying I love to share, just to watch the puzzles form on listeners' faces as they try to decipher the message. It goes like this: "One dog, you have a dog. Two dogs, you have half a dog. Three dogs, you have no dog at all."

The point, of course, is that due to pack behavior, the closeness of a human's relationship with a companion dog depends on how many dogs there are. When there are several, you don't have one-on-one relationships – you live with a pack. My neighbor observes this behavior in her husband and his two grown sons, with whom he is very close. When they're away, she has a husband. When one son is present, she says she has roughly half a husband and when all three are together, she laments (but with a smile), that she really has no husband at all.

Even though I work with people day in and day out, am socially adept and enjoy interaction with others, I'm an introvert by nature. That just means I get my energy by being alone or with one very close, significant other. I expend energy in my work and in social interactions, and need time in nature or with one close (and quiet) friend to recharge. Extroverts, on the other hand, gain energy by being with people. I often tease a strongly extroverted colleague about the time she told me, in all seriousness, that she couldn't wait to relax on a Jimmy Buffet cruise with 200 of her closest friends. "200 close friends?" I exclaimed. I could not imagine having that many friends (though this was before Facebook), let alone consider being with all of them at once "relaxing."

This introvert/extrovert concept is complex, because we need different things from groups than from our one-on-one relationships. In this world of never-enough-time, I tend to covet and protect time alone with special pals, even to the point of (I confess), sometimes resenting when well-meaning others join us. As an introvert, I tend to let the "pack" do its pack thing, with me on the fringes as a lone wolf. I can easily lose connection and drift away into my own thoughts while they carry on as a unit.

Susan Cain's bestseller, *Quiet: The Power of Introverts In A World That Can't Stop Talking,* does a beautiful job of helping introverts understand themselves a bit better and nudges their extroverted friends, partners and colleagues to consider a different way of interacting with them. You can assess your own preferences with her quiz or many other instruments that measure these qualities.

If you need the absence of connection, the solitude of your choosing, to build the energy to connect with important others in your life, consider the choices you are making. Do you go along with crowd, later feeling exhausted or even resentful that your bucket is empty? Or do you make time for quiet, alone or with a quiet confidant? Honoring these core needs contributes to the quality of our lives.

If you need the absence of connection, the solitude of your choosing, to build the energy to connect with important others in your life, consider the choices you are making. Do you go along with crowd, later feeling exhausted or even resentful that your bucket is empty? Or do you make time for quiet, alone or with a quiet confidant? Honoring these core needs contributes to the quality of our lives.

Reflections on Solitude

Putting Self First

"I am the most important person in my life right now."

Lately it seems I have less time and more demands on that precious time. Sound familiar? When I recently shared this lament with a trusted confidant, she asked me to do something that on the surface sounded simple. Her request? "State the following, then tell me how it feels to you. 'I am the most important person in my life right now.'"

Well, it felt incongruent. Even though I believe that unless I care for myself first I cannot possibly care for important others in my life, I sure did not feel it in the midst of my all-too-busy day.

My friend's question sparked thoughts about the great equilibrium of giving and receiving. It can be out of balance literally, or in our heads. Rejuvenating activities, gratitude or compliments from those we love, as well as simple acts of kindness shown to us, all produce healing energy. Are we allowing enough of that in our lives?

Consider the literal examples. We can starve ourselves by constantly doing for others, never taking the time to replenish in whatever way creates true enjoyment. We can surround ourselves with people who take only (energy vampires, as Dr. Judith Orloff describes them), rather than spend time with people who know the beautiful dance of give and take. If you are one of these givers, you probably recognize the toll it takes on you, and, most likely, the things that you seek — acceptance, purpose, love — are elusive.

More insidious is the type of starvation that is made up in our minds. In this scenario we do a lot and are offered a lot, but — we don't notice what's coming back to us because our metal drive is so focused on the next task. I get caught in this mind trap often. I am blessed with a loving husband as well as friends, clients and animal companions who give me as much or more than I give out. But often I miss these precious gifts because the to-do lists in my brain trick me into believing I have no time for them.

The affirmation offered by my friend – "I am the most important person in my life right now" – was profound. Once I made that statement, I was forced to re-focus on the present moment. What I was doing did not change, but the way I did it changed significantly. I came back alive, appreciating the small and beautiful give and take in the interactions of life.

As I moved through the next several days, I did, as usual, a great deal for others. What I provide the people and animals I love brings me great joy. And I en-joy that work when I come from a place of integrity in myself and my capacity.

So, take the challenge given to me. Can you love yourself enough to care for those you love?

So, take the challenge given to me…

Can you love yourself enough to care for those you love?

Reflections on Putting Yourself First

Letting Go

This past weekend was very special for my family. Our foster Husky dog, Phoenix, went to his forever home.

Three weeks ago, late on Saturday night, I got an urgent email from a worker at the county shelter. They had brought in a half-dead Siberian Husky who had been attacked by dogs. He faced a certain death if not claimed, immediately, by a rescue group. Fortunately, I was able to reach two such angels Carrie Singer, the founder of Animal Guardian Network and Marie Peck, the founder of The Fetch Foundation, and they arranged for me to retrieve him to the safety of my home. It turns out his wounds were serious but treatable, and he was a pup, less than a year old.

Happily, through anything-but-coincidental events, a family came along to adopt "Phoenix." I had bonded with him as he healed, and shed tears as I prepared him for his journey.

That day I was reminded of the fleeting relationships we have with some people (as well as animals) in our lives. Of course, most of us are all blessed with life-long friendships and family bonds. And we also meet and connect with people who come and go. These brief connections offer us gifts in the form of life lessons or a simple helping hand when needed, and they take gifts from us. Have you ever wondered about the purpose of a transitory relationship? They're easier to release when it seems we gave more than we were given, or when there was more hurt than happiness. But there are others that we try to hang on to, in order to recreate the magic after the magic has faded.

Consider this. There are people who enter our lives in pure synchronicity, for a clear and finite purpose, then exit. The purpose of the relationship may be ours or theirs, and we often don't ever fully understand the "why" of it all. The important thing is the memory, the life lesson, or the gift exchanged.

In the animal rescue world, there are people called "foster failures." These kind folks take in animals to foster, but cannot give them up – eventually rendering themselves unable to foster because their kennel is full, so to speak. For many homeless and helpless animals, it's a blessing there is so much needed compassion. In human relationships, it's a bit different. Some people need to be allowed to "fly away" and find the right connections for the next leg of their journey.

I know in my heart that sweet Phoenix belongs with his new family, even as I miss his sparkling blues eyes and loving demeanor. And, I know what we both meant to each other's lives, however brief the interlude.

Do you need to free the spirit of another to *travel* his or her own path?

Reflections on Letting Go

Living Through It

It's been almost a year since my sweet friend Amigo, a sparkling white Siberian Husky who looked like a pup until he died, left this earth. One late January day I was hiking up a steep desert mountain with him, a consummate athlete, even at 12 plus years. The next day I was told his liver was failing and his prospects were grave.

I'm supposed to be an unofficial expert on the grief we experience upon the loss of a special animal companion. After all, our book *Erik's Hope* chronicles, among other things, the dark night of the soul I struggled through years ago when my dog Erik passed, as well as the renewal of hope and faith I experienced as a result of surrendering to the intensity of the ordeal.

Amigo's illness and death were a test of my faith, as well as my integrity. If I truly believed what I had written, that I now know the spirit survives death, this experience would be different. It was.

The watershed visit to the veterinarian is etched in my psyche like an indelible image. Upon receiving the diagnosis, I felt faint. The room began to spin as my mind tried to comprehend – and reject – what I was being told. How could this be? How could twelve years have passed since that wonderful day when the pup Amigo entered my life, when the spirit of his predecessor Erik brought us healing joy? And how was I going to come to terms with the mortality of this particular unique expression of life, a lone wolf personality, a self-confident being so stealth and mysterious few even knew him as I did?

Many of you reading this have had the experience of receiving shocking news that changes your world, for a time or forever. Relationships quickly transform; partners become caregivers, children parent their elders. There's a common denominator to our experiences. You just do what you have to do. One foot in front of the other, one step informs the next. When Amigo became ill, there was little time for pondering the metaphysical meaning of it all. That would have to wait.

For three months, I tried, with much expert assistance, to save my friend. And even as he became increasingly frail, we savored each day together, finding simple joy in simple presence. Maybe I had indeed learned something from his life.

A day in April marked a profound change. Amigo was not going to heal despite my (and his?) prayers. On that sad day, I knew I could endure what was to come. I knew that I would love and comfort him in all the ways he deserved, help him depart, and while quite challenging, I knew I would endure and survive the pain of his loss. From the depths of my being, I knew what I learned from Erik was real: Love never dies. It changes form, a process filled with wrenching human ache – but it does not die.

Lately, I find myself recalling what was happening each day one year ago, and reliving those feelings. They pass more gently and more quickly now, smoothed and molded by the experiences of this difficult but miraculous year.

If your spirits are or ever have been saddened by a loss in your life – any kind of loss – you might relate to this paradox, this enduring faith that stands beside painful grief. Allow the feelings of sadness, despair or anger when they come. An open channel for emotion also allows the love to re-enter – eventually, and fully.

If your spirits are or ever have been saddened by a loss in your life – any kind of loss – you might relate to this paradox, this enduring faith that stands beside painful grief. Allow the feelings of sadness, despair or anger when they come.

An open channel for emotion also allows the love to re-enter – eventually, and fully.

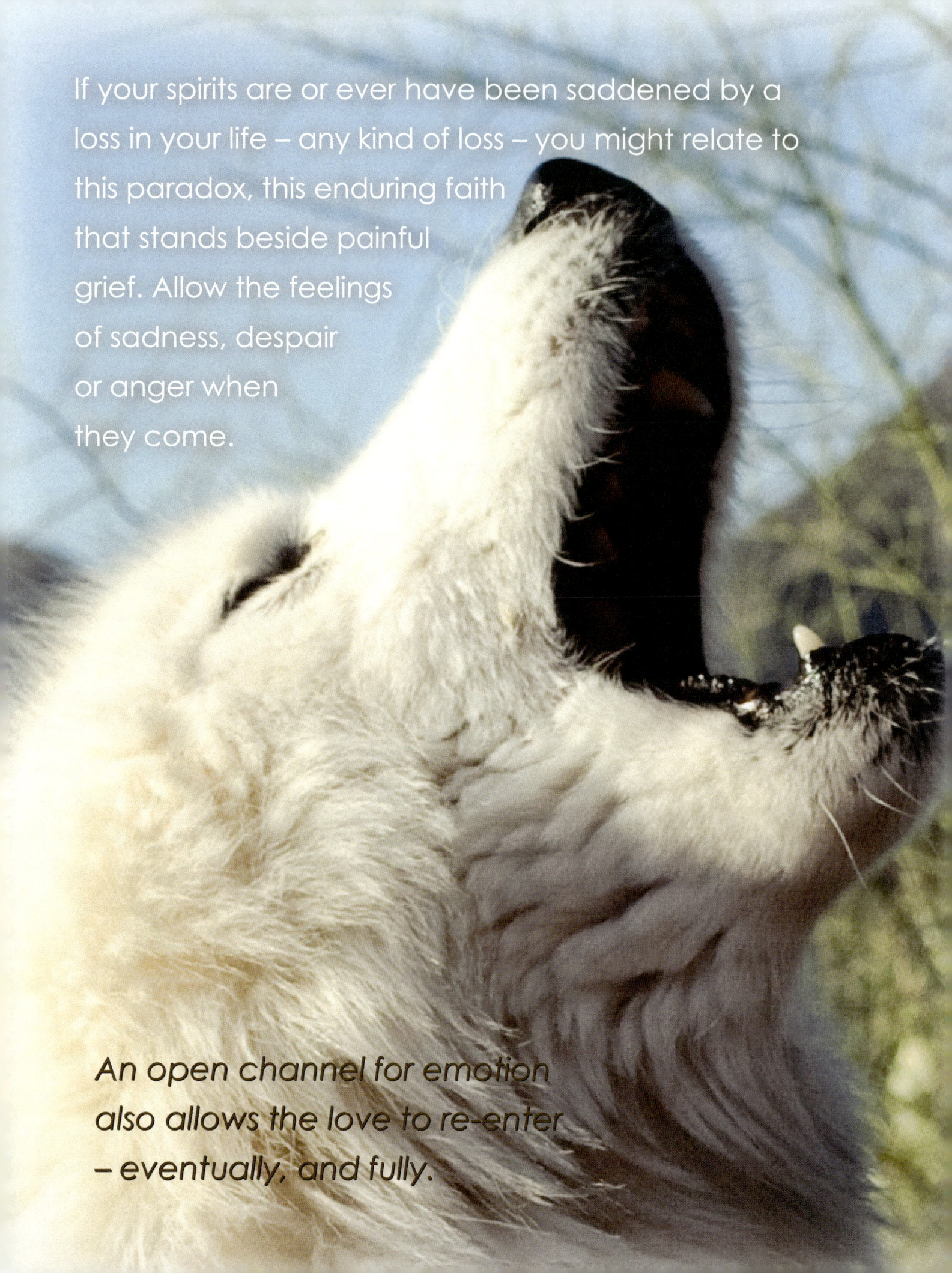

Reflections on Living Through It

Transform Judgment

Lately, I've spent much of my time working one-on-one with people from very diverse walks of life and with quite different needs. Even with the varied backdrops, a theme keeps reappearing: judgment. Self-judgment, judgment of others – that subtle process of forming an opinion that leads to even more subtle and often unconscious behavior directed at those we judge.

My work has always been about helping people change behaviors that are unproductive (and even destructive) in their relationships. Behaviors are tangible; they can be seen and heard. We can stop and listen to ourselves, or receive feedback from others, then make a choice to do something different and better. But if you have ever tried to act or react differently toward a situation or person that "pushes your buttons," you know how difficult changing your own behavior can be.

Imagine one of those button-pushing people in your own life. Recall a touchy situation and then try to think of something you could have done or said differently to create a more positive outcome. You may or may not be able to think of something. Even if you can, doing it is a whole different story. Right?

It's hard to change how we act or behave because, if we really analyze it, we think our behavior is justified. This mind-trap is almost certainly being driven by a feeling, one that often goes unnoticed.

In a world where being busy is valued, rapid decision making is expected, and multi-tasking is rewarded, who has time to truly become present and feel? But that's the key to the kingdom, so to speak. Lack of this simple presence can result in misunderstanding, or even disaster.

So take time out right now and get present. Take a breath and notice the sights and sounds around you. Recall the incident with the button-pusher. How does it feel to you? As you recall a past confrontation or presume a future interaction, what feeling do you have? What motive is driving you? Are you judging yourself or another, and if so, is it really fair and accurate? With new perspective comes transformation.

As I've done this work with clients (and myself) these last few weeks, we've unraveled many small mysteries that have led to breakthroughs in thinking and acting. Impatience led to inclusion, inadequacy morphed into acceptance, and a motive to highlight wrongdoing was converted into motivation to solve a problem. Small and incremental, one step leads to another.

Here's another tip: be gentle on yourselves. When we take responsibility for how we behave in connection with others, there's a tendency for more self-judgment. True responsibility includes conscientiousness in how we regard – vs. judge – ourselves.

"Taking responsibility for
your beliefs and judgments
gives you the power to
change them."

— *Byron Katie*

Reflections on Judgment

Who Are You?

Want to know how to get what you need from the relationships you value in life? Know what you need. And, knowing what you need results from knowing who you are.

In my experience, an essential price of admission for healthy, satisfying relationships with others is a clear and grounded sense of self. I'm not talking about self-indulgence or selfishness. I'm referring to the settled sense that comes from knowing and loving the uniqueness that is you.

As a coach, I utilize instruments that help me quickly (and painlessly) assess clients' core drivers, productive behaviors and the consequences of unmet needs. When revealing the results of these assessment tools, I'm sometimes met by a distinct response, a bewildered astonishment that I could reveal aspects of their personality so carefully hidden away. Often they themselves had not consciously considered these traits, but when faced with the data, they have a whole new world of choices. Recently I met with a new client over dinner to review the information I had compiled, a combination of feedback from others and her Birkman Report, an instrument which reveals elements of the personality. At the end of the evening, she remarked, "Well, it was very enlightening to have dinner with someone who knows me better than I know myself."

While these tools are quite helpful, the fact is you don't need a report to tell you who you are. You know when you are your best, most productive self. You know the activities and people from whom you gain energy vs. being depleted. You know what makes you feel most alive.

Do you let your true self be known in your day-to-day interactions with significant others? Is there some aspect of your personality – some core need you have – that's hidden away? There's a cost to holding back. At a minimum, when we don't acknowledge and reveal who we are and what we need, we miss the most basic satisfaction in life. At worst, we find ourselves entangled in personal and professional relationships that can be destructive to body or psyche.

A relationship is a product of the interaction of two parts. Changing your awareness alone can shift everything. My client has managed to change the perception of her work team by revealing herself in day-to-day interactions, a "self" she had to acknowledge first and foremost.

What is it that you need from a key relationship in your life? Take responsibility by naming it, then examine what you are doing (or not) to nurture that quality. What can you do to show up as who you are?

What is it that you need from a key relationship in your life? Take responsibility by naming it, then examine what you are doing (or not) to nurture that quality.

What can you do to show up as who you are?

Reflections on Knowing Who You Are

The Need for Renewal

Recently, I led a workshop with a team of people who are driven, dedicated – and stretched thin. I began our work with two questions: "How do you feel right now?" and "What do you need?"

Almost everyone replied with some version of the following: "I feel very tired, and I need rest and rejuvenation." As they spoke, I secretly related. It had been a long and exhausting week for me as well, and I was looking forward to a weekend of play with friends who were visiting us, a rare three-day respite from the demands of life.

Even as I pushed forward that day, I realized that I was fatigued, and in need of a good night's sleep. But there was more. I felt a longing for connection with people who enjoy and value the things I do. I wanted to be outdoors, enjoying the wonderland that is my desert in March. And I longed to be with my loving and goofy dogs, a pack that includes a foster Husky. For me, rest can be active. It's a time when I can turn off the noise of my mind and focus on the experience at hand – an enjoyable one.

How do you feel right now? What do you need? Close your eyes, take a deep breath, and feel the answers to the questions. Do you feel stress or fatigue? Do you have a longing for some enjoyable experience that has been missing from your life?

If you have no shortage of things to do, it may seem as if there's no time for "me" time, rest time or play time. It is, of course, a matter of prioritization. If you're telling yourself a story about how you can't possibly do the thing you long to do, consider the cost of depriving yourself. Recreation is defined as "refreshment of health or spirits by relaxation and enjoyment."

Rest and recreation does not have to take a long time or cost a lot of money. Many years ago, I regularly dreamed about fun activities with friends during particularly stressful times. While I couldn't call upon those dreams at will, they conveyed a valuable message that I was working too much and playing too little. Life coach Martha Beck offers practical advice for adding more laughter, play and connection to your life in her book, *The Joy Diet*. Intentional Resting's Dan Howard promotes active resting and teaches simple tools for calling upon a restful state in the midst of everyday activities.

This past weekend, I played hard and laughed heartily. We took long hikes, enjoyed fine food and wine, and howled with the Husky dogs. I'm rejuvenated and ready to meet the challenges life has in store this week. And, the people around me will benefit from my more relaxed state of being..

What do you need to rest and recharge in a positive way? Whether you have three days, three hours or three minutes – take action – and enjoy the rewards.

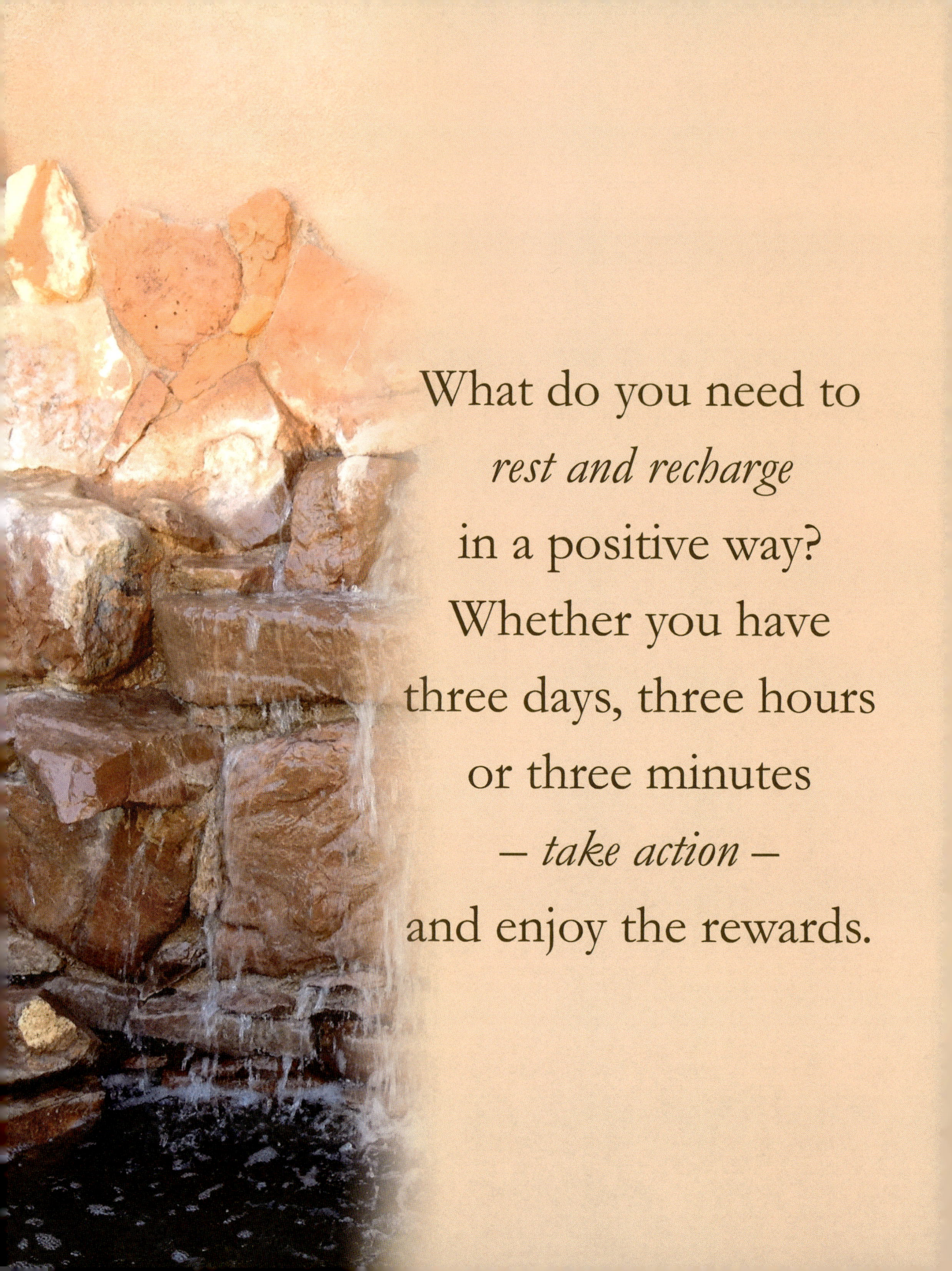

What do you need to
rest and recharge
in a positive way?
Whether you have
three days, three hours
or three minutes
— *take action* —
and enjoy the rewards.

Reflections on Renewal

The Personal Plus of Positive Intent

As an observer of human behavior – sometimes student and sometimes teacher – I marvel at the fact that there are so many simple and reliable tools for making relationships of all kinds easier. Even when aware of these tools, we so often fail to employ them in the very circumstances that count.

One example is a simple mental model called "positive intent." I've been working to assume positive intent quite a bit these days, as a way to ease the stresses and frustrations of a busy life. It's so easy to become irritated by others' supposed shortcomings or to take personally the minor transgressions seemingly committed on purpose to make life difficult. The principle of positive intent requires us to ask one simple question prior to judging, assuming motive for, or reacting to another person's behavior. "What possible, positive reason does he or she have for doing or saying that?"

It doesn't matter what the answer is. The very moment you have an answer, no matter how preposterous it seems, something shifts. Something very big.

There's a well known illustration of the principle in Stephen's Covey's blockbuster title, *The Seven Habits of Highly Effective People.* In short, as a passenger in a crowded subway, Covey becomes irritated at a father who is not disciplining his unruly children. When he gathers the courage to ask the man to intervene, the father tells him they are all returning from the hospital where their mother (his wife), has just died. Covey experiences an instantaneous paradigm shift. Suddenly his irritation pales in comparison to the man's grief.

The truth of positive intent is one of the toughest things for our egos to swallow. Yet once we assume there might be a reason for another's behavior that, while perhaps misguided, to them makes some kind of sense, we are then free. Free of being violated, persecuted or even mildly disrespected. Suddenly, our thoughts and feelings are independent of the influence of other's actions. What a break this gives us, in a world in which we are bombarded by input, some welcome and some not.

We can all assume positive intent in daily interactions with everyone from strangers to casual acquaintances. The benefit is a bit less stress, a tad more peace in our hearts.

Can you assume positive intent in the most challenging of your relationships? There lies an opportunity that just might transform those relationships. When we think differently, we act differently. When we act differently, others re-act in new ways. Pat your ego gently on the shoulder and try something new – you might reap a surprising reward.

Can you assume positive intent in the most challenging of your relationships? There lies an opportunity that just might transform those relationships. When we think differently, we act differently. When we act differently, others re-act in new ways. Pat your ego gently on the shoulder and try something new – you might reap a surprising reward.

Reflections on Positive Intent

Transition's Destination

Being "in transition" implies you have left one place (physically, mentally or emotionally) and have not yet arrived in another. And one of the more daunting challenges associated with transition is not knowing where you are going. I don't know about you, but while I am enjoying the journey, I want to have a destination on the horizon.

The process of defining a destination, an intended outcome, sounds simple – though we can make it into a complex science project.

I've never cared for mind benders, those frustrating puzzles that make your brain hurt. Yet I've spent a good portion of my life puzzling over so-called universal principles that feel just like mind benders. I'm referring to profound revelations uttered by philosophers and gurus that you just know are The Truth, yet are paradoxical and seem hard to live by in practical terms.

One such head scratcher is the concept of detachment. According to this gem of wisdom, we must set a clear and compelling vision, then…let it go. The idea is that with attachment, our fears and obsessions will muddy the pure intent, contriving all manner of disaster and plotting contingencies to prevent such. This focus on the details can be exacerbated when one is in transition, because it feels as though all we control is the minutiae.

Does this "law of detachment" mean we should stop wanting what we say we want? No, no – and therein sits the conundrum. The problem often lies in defining what we want. Often what we say we want is just a means of getting to some higher-level, often unexpressed, goal. What we get attached to is the mechanism – this house, this job, this relationship – and we miss all of the beautiful opportunities that show up along the way.

In your heart of hearts, what do you know you truly want? And, what will having that bring you? The answer to the second question is, in all likelihood, what you truly desire. The rest is just method or means, the detailed how-to that your clever mind has calculated. These instructions we issue to the universe squelch our creative wisdom and limit the innate potential available to all. Most of the time, we're not in charge of the how-to's anyway. Have you ever looked back after some miraculous achievement and wondered how it all came together? W.H. Murray's famous statement says it all: "The moment one definitely commits oneself, then providence moves too."

Look forward. Craft your vision, paint a picture of your heart's desire. See it, feel it, imagine it come to life. Then let it be. Go about your day, enjoying each precious and fleeting moment. You might be surprised at what happens around the next bend.

Look forward. Craft your vision, paint a picture of your heart's desire. See it, feel it, imagine it come to life. Then let it be. Go about your day, enjoying each precious and fleeting moment.

You might be surprised at what happens next.

Reflections on Defining Your Destination

The Story of This Very Moment

If – perhaps especially if – you're in transition, you are writing the story of your life right now, with each thought you have and each breath you take. And, re-telling the story of your life requires examining the story you are living today.

Many years ago I was living in a seemingly foreign place, away from my husband and four-legged family, finishing out a commitment to a job while anticipating a move to start my business. I was both exhilarated and terrified about my future, and anxious to be finished with my current assignment. And, I was lonely.

In hindsight, I learned a lesson. I had put my life "on hold," working too much at a job that was unfulfilling, longing to be with my family, and obsessing about the future. Toward the end of the eight month period, I met a young family who invited me into their life. This brief experience helped me recognize that I had squandered the precious present moment far too long. Rather than engaging in life where I was, I had been living in a world of "what-if's," an uncomfortable mental state in which I was trying to hold on to what had really ended while unable to step fully into my future.

Change expert William Bridges suggests that in any transition, we experience a stage of letting go, then a stage of neutrality in which nothing feels grounded or clear; finally, those two stages are followed by a period of orienting to new beginnings. I suggest, while these are natural stages we must pass through, we can continue to live the story of a meaningful life even inside the so-called neutral zone. It's as simple as showing up.

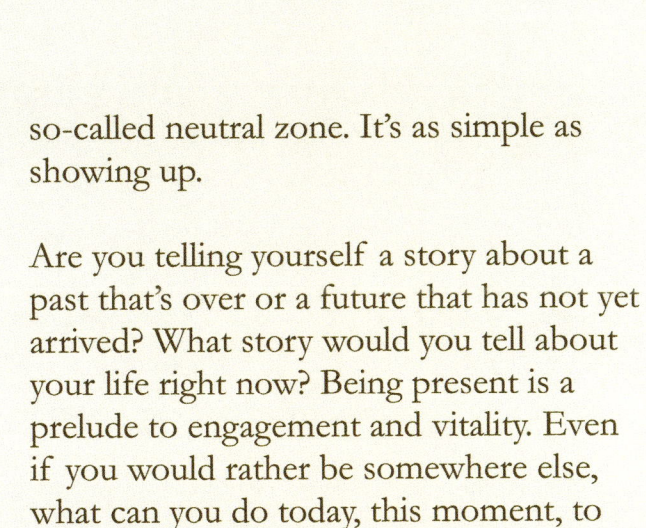

Are you telling yourself a story about a past that's over or a future that has not yet arrived? What story would you tell about your life right now? Being present is a prelude to engagement and vitality. Even if you would rather be somewhere else, what can you do today, this moment, to come alive again?

The fleeting present moment is filled with potential opportunities and possibilities, yet we often miss them because we're consumed by a mind cluttered with thoughts about the past or the future. Stop – then look, listen and feel. Are you willing to engage in the precious opportunity before you?

The fleeting present moment is filled with potential opportunities and possibilities, yet we often miss them because we're consumed by a mind cluttered with thoughts about the past or the future. Stop – then look, listen and feel. Are you willing to engage in the precious opportunity before you?

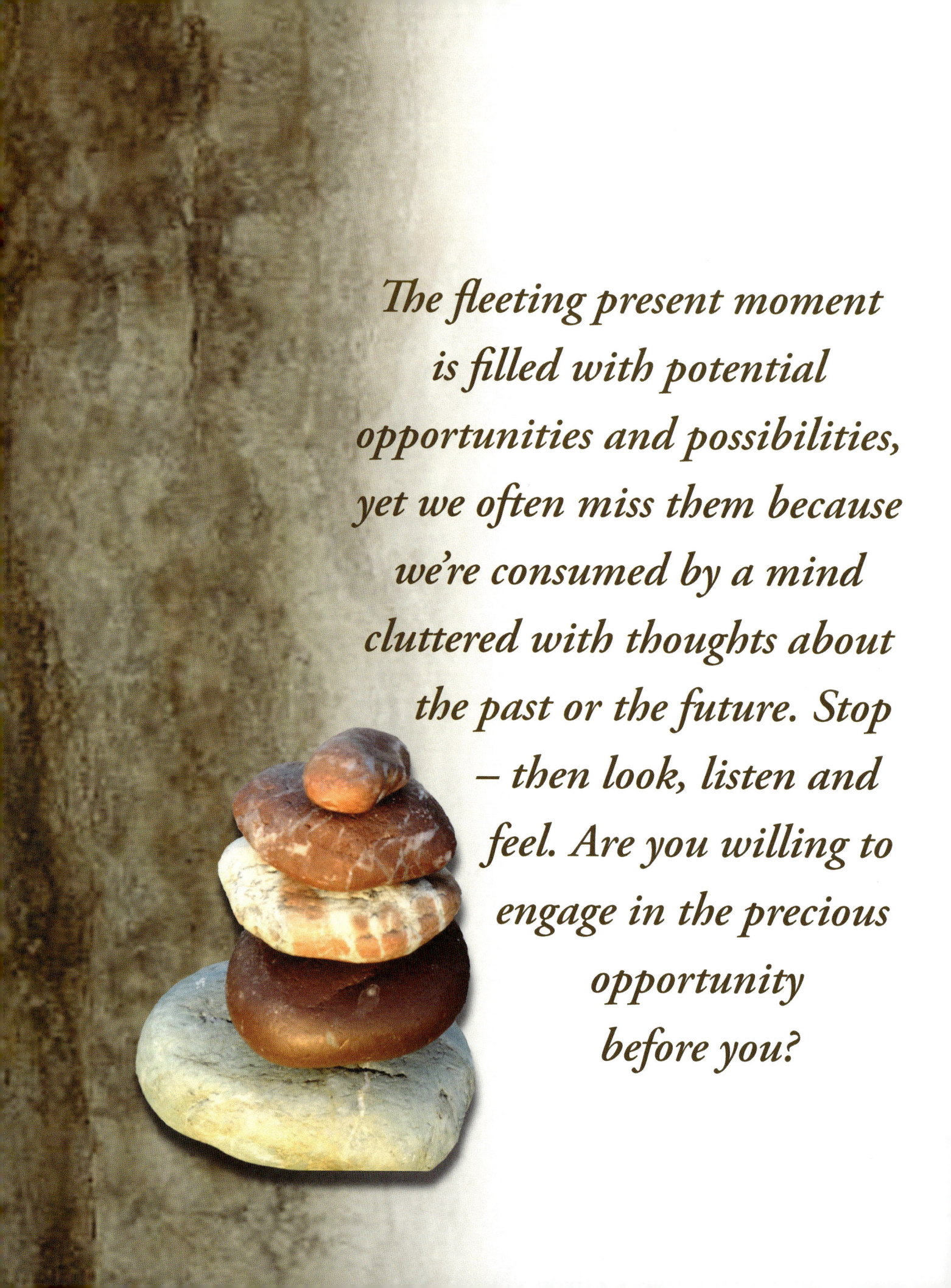

Reflections on This Very Moment

Just Chill

As I write this, I am officially on vacation. I am in Cambria, California, an idyllic haven that offers my family and me a unique sort of respite, a place to "chill out" figuratively as well as literally, given that it's also a cool escape from the blistering Arizona summer.

I strive for peace and quiet amidst the busyness of my life. Yet the world is not quiet. That is not a judgment, rather it is an observation. Whether one is a public servant, a public figure – or even a monk – this "disquiet" can seep into the psyche, creating discord that impacts the quality of our lives and those we care about and interact with daily.

In the past, I have written of the importance of rest and renewal. And, as is so often the case, I have observed a theme this past week: A dearth of rest. So many people are starved for a break, for peace and for release. The definition of rest is broad. It can mean temporary cessation from an activity as well as relief or freedom from disquiet or disturbance. Rest includes recreation, and it can literally re-create our outlook, equipping us with renewed drive and energy to use as we choose.

Some of us "rest" in motion…through vigorous physical activity, or an active break from routine. Others need stillness and contemplation. The idea of a nap or an afternoon under a beach umbrella may satisfy some and not others. For me, the simple absence of a schedule provides supreme rest.

We've been resting in Cambria each summer for the last six years. On the first day of our first trip there, Arthur and I were having lunch at a wonderful sidewalk table at a Cambria classic, the Indigo Moon. Our dogs, Whisper and Amigo, were with us. Just as our server approached, another vacationing dog passed by our table. Whisper, the Malamute, tends to challenge other dogs, and this was no exception. The server looked her straight in the eye and cut her off mid-growl. "Chill doggie," she said calmly. "This is Cambria." Amazingly, both dogs "chilled." From that day forward, time in Cambria came to represent a time to take a deep breath and relax.

Maybe you too can visit Cambria, in person or in your dreams.
Until then, just chill.

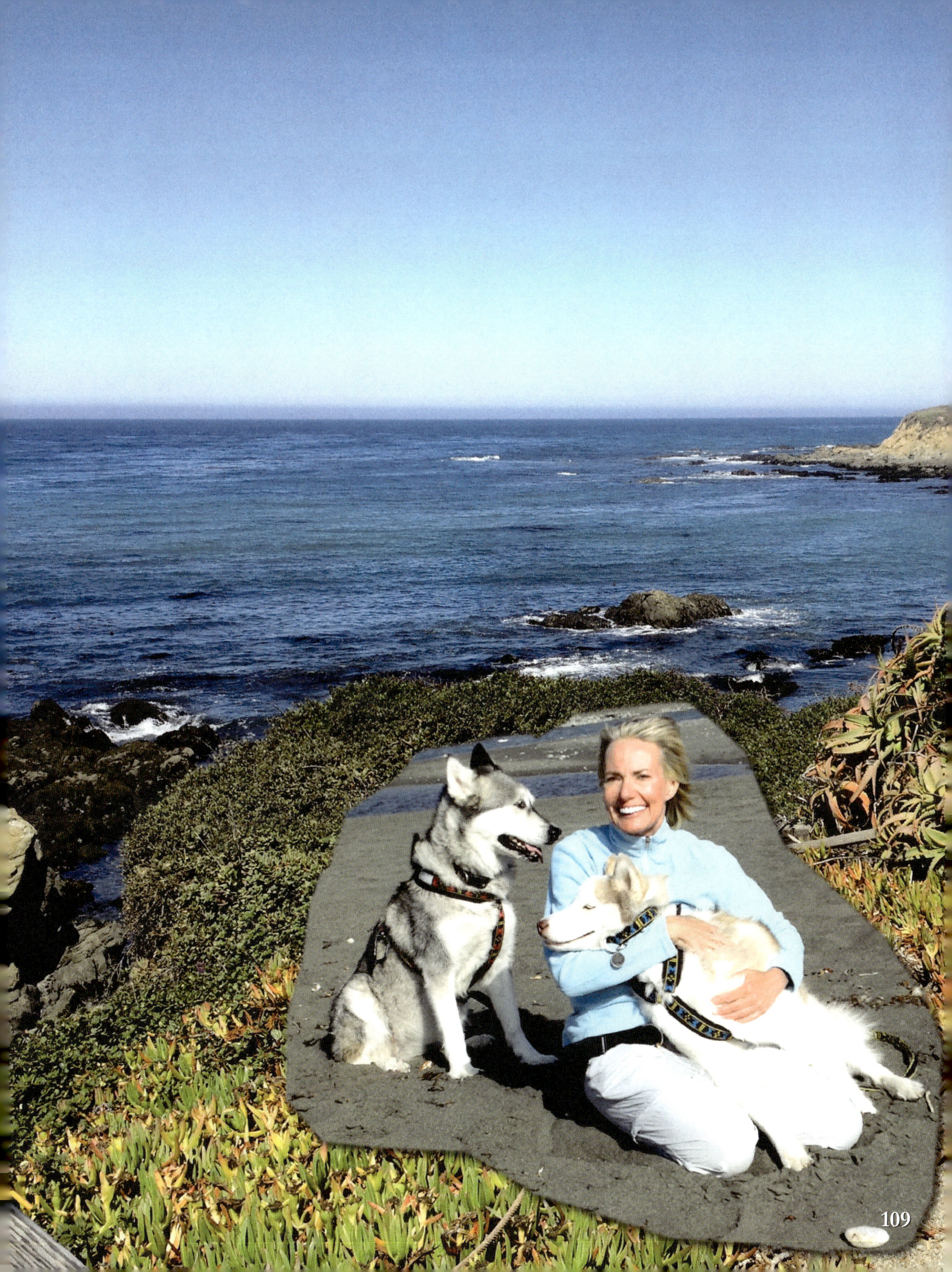

Just Chill...

Reflections on Chilling

We See What We Expect

I've collected rocks all of my life. I'm as drawn to unique, rough stones on a hiking path as I am to beautiful crystal mineral specimens on display in specialty shops. And since moving to the desert 12 years ago, I have been picking up heart-shaped stones of varied size and composition from the many hiking trails I frequent. In recent years I've expanded my search to beaches where we vacation, and occasionally friends bring me specimens from their travels.

My home and property hold my rather large collection of "heart rocks," as I call them. Recently I gathered them together to create a photograph for this book cover. As I shared that photo with friends, I was often asked, "How do you find these?" Where do you get them? One even asked, "Are these natural or purchased in a store?" My response was simple. "They are everywhere…just open your eyes." These questions and my answer remind me of an age old principle: We see what we expect to see.

Friends who hike with me, neighbors as well as visitors from other states, understand this principle well. We need only to set an intention to look for and find heart rocks, and they show up, literally beneath our feet. They were always there of course, but until we believe they're there and then look for them, they don't "show up."

Psychologists say we actively construct our perception of reality. By the time information reaches our brain, it's combined with information from past experiences, skewing our perception. Maria Konnikova, who blogs about the psychology of decision making, says, "It's comforting to think our brains work like a camera," though in fact that's not the case. Inputs are subject to interpretation.

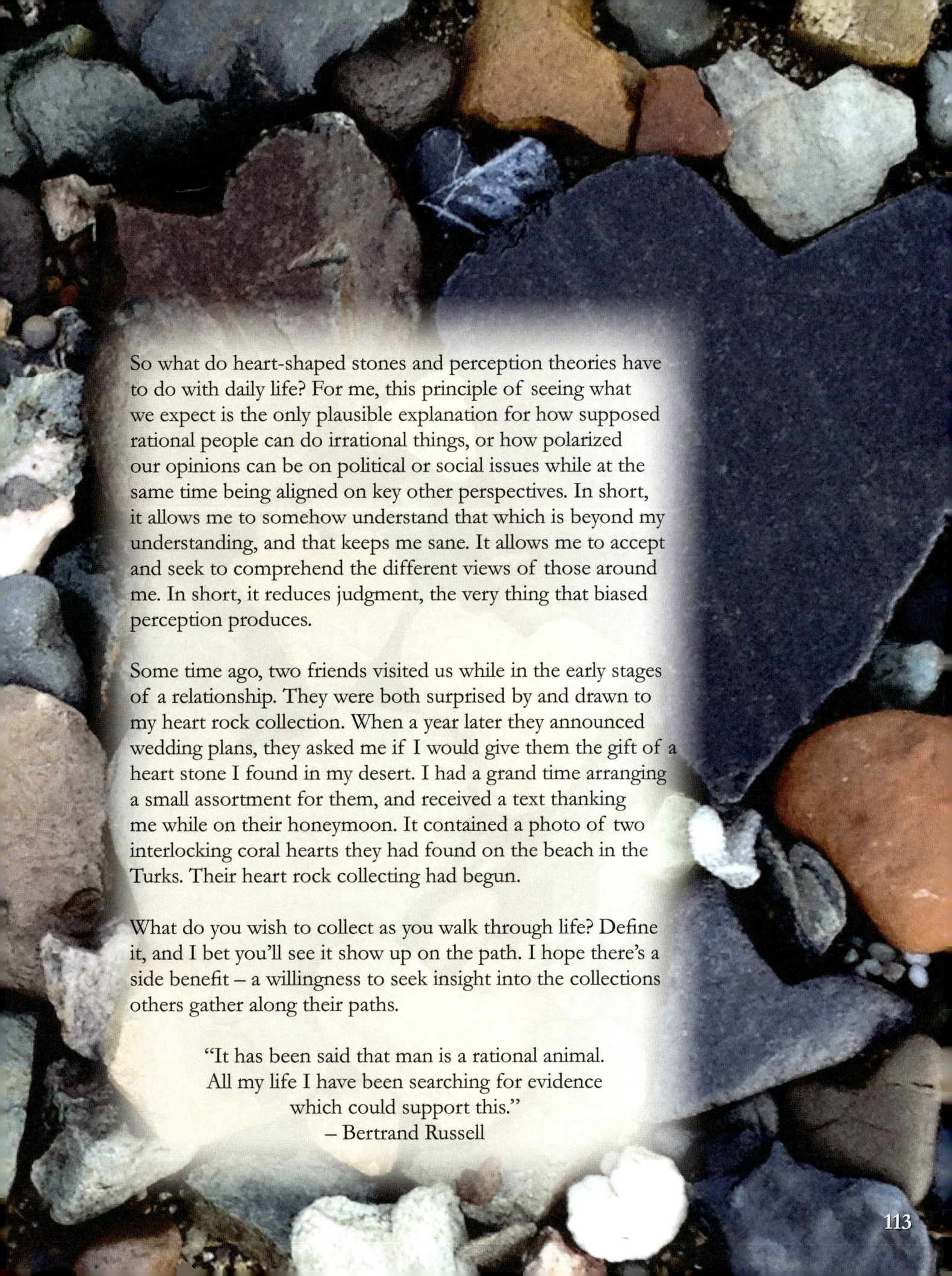

So what do heart-shaped stones and perception theories have to do with daily life? For me, this principle of seeing what we expect is the only plausible explanation for how supposed rational people can do irrational things, or how polarized our opinions can be on political or social issues while at the same time being aligned on key other perspectives. In short, it allows me to somehow understand that which is beyond my understanding, and that keeps me sane. It allows me to accept and seek to comprehend the different views of those around me. In short, it reduces judgment, the very thing that biased perception produces.

Some time ago, two friends visited us while in the early stages of a relationship. They were both surprised by and drawn to my heart rock collection. When a year later they announced wedding plans, they asked me if I would give them the gift of a heart stone I found in my desert. I had a grand time arranging a small assortment for them, and received a text thanking me while on their honeymoon. It contained a photo of two interlocking coral hearts they had found on the beach in the Turks. Their heart rock collecting had begun.

What do you wish to collect as you walk through life? Define it, and I bet you'll see it show up on the path. I hope there's a side benefit – a willingness to seek insight into the collections others gather along their paths.

> "It has been said that man is a rational animal. All my life I have been searching for evidence which could support this."
> – Bertrand Russell

What do you wish to collect as you walk through life? Define it, and I bet you'll see it show up on the path.

Reflections on Seeing What You Expect

About the Author

Morningstar ventures

Morningstar Ventures, Andrea Chilcote's consulting company, provides business consulting services in the areas of leadership development, executive development, team performance and personal change, as well as program design and implementation.

The no-nonsense, results oriented approach to leadership development is personal, unique to each organization and individual.

www.morningstarventures.com
P.O. Box 1723 – Cave Creek, AZ 85327
480-575-8533

Andrea Chilcote, CEO of Morningstar Ventures, is an author, executive coach, and leadership development expert. She demonstrates practical knowledge of the issues and concerns people are facing at this difficult time. She has a keen skilled and intuitive ability to facilitate transformational change in individuals and organizations, and her writing offers this opportunity to the reader.

She has created numerous popular learning programs, and has published a fictional work, *Erik's Hope: The Leash That Led Me To Freedom,* based on her own life memoir. She has authored diverse articles on the nature of change, leadership development and communication.

Andrea lives in Cave Creek, Arizona with her husband, dogs and horses.

This Very Moment, by Andrea Chilcote is available for purchase on Amazon.com and BarnesandNoble.com

ERIK'S HOPE: *The Leash That Led Me to Freedom* is a fictional account based on the true story of Andrea Chilcote's transformational journey, assisted by her beloved dog, Erik. The book chronicles Andrea's shift from a high-performing professional with little regard for matters of the heart to a passionate and caring expert in personal leadership change and growth.

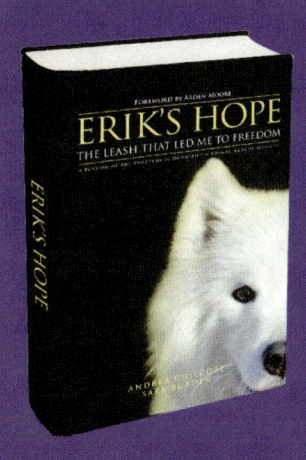

Erik's rescue from the Phoenix animal shelter is far from happenstance, though Andrea could not comprehend the impact of her decision to adopt the mangy wolf-dog. He's a handful from the start, immediately testing her readiness to fully engage in life's joys and trials.

Erik's Hope, by Andrea Chilcote and Sara Burden is available for purchase on Amazon.com and BarnesandNoble.com

www.erikshope.com

Andrea Chilcote
Executive Coach – Author
Leadership Development Consultant

follow Andrea's blog and ongoing musings:
erikshope.wordpress.com

Acknowledgements

The content of this collection is drawn from my life and my work. My daily interactions with family, friends, clients and colleagues provide the subject matter. Some of you are named. I have changed details to allow many of you to remain anonymous, though you probably recognize your own story. I am grateful to all of you for the ways in which you enrich my life, and for allowing me to use your stories to help others along the way. A loving thank you to my husband, Arthur, for allowing me to share details of our wonderful life together.

A special thank you to friend and photographer David Culp, www.DavidCulpPhotography.com, for the use of the photos on pages 25, 73, 81 and 82. Thank you Brenda Seelbach for the hours of artistic design you contributed and Beth Ballmann for the early morning hours spent staging the cover shot. To all who have given me gifts of heart stones: can you find yours among the others? Susanne Wilson, I am grateful to you and Whisper for the conversation so perfect for "Mirror Mirror" on page 24.

References

Jennifer Kahnweiler, *The Introverted Leader: Building on Your Quiet Strength* (California, Berrett-Koehler, 2009).
Susan Cain, *Quiet: The Power of Introverts in a World That Can't Stop Talking* (New York, Crown, 2012).
Stephen Covey, *The Seven Habits of Highly Effective People* (New York, Simon and Schuster, 1998).
Gregory Rineberg, *WordPower Blog* (www.babeled.com/2009/01/08/word-power-resolution, 2009).
Grantland Rice, *Base-Ball Ballads* (New York, Mcfarland & Co Inc Pub 2004).
Chris Peterson and Martin Seligman, *Character Strengths and Virtues* (New York, Oxford University Press, 2004).
Chris Argyris, *Action Science* (New York, Putnam & Smith, 1985).
Martha Beck, *The Joy Diet: 10 Daily Practices for a Happier Life* (New York, Crown Archetype, 2003).
Dan Howard, *Intentional Resting Audio,* (New York, 2004).
William Bridges, *Transitions: Making Sense of Life's Changes* (Massachusetts, Da Capo Press, 2004).
Byron Katie, www.thework.com.
Maria Konnikova, www.mariakonnikova.com/blog.
T.S. Eliot, *The Four Quartets, Burnt Norton* (Florida, Harcourt, Inc., 1946).
Sarah Ban Breathnach, *Simple Abundance: A Daybook of Comfort and Joy* (New York, Warner Books, Inc., 1995).
Mahatma Gandhi, *Collected Works of Mahatma Gandhi, Volume 13, Chapter 153, page 241*.
Rick Ross, *The Fifth Discipline Fieldbook* (New York, Crown Business, 1994).
W.H. Murray, *The Scottish Himalayan Expedition* (London, 1951).
Cesar Millan and Melissa Jo Peltier, *Cesar's Way* (New York, Crown Publishing, , 2006).
Judith Orloff, M.D., *Emotional Freedom* (New York, Three Rivers Press, 2009).
Eckhart Tolle, *A New Earth: Awakening to Your Life's Purpose* (New York, Penguin Group, 2005).
Mike Dooley, *Notes from the Universe: New Perspectives from an Old Friend* (New York, Atria Books, 2003).
Bertrand Russell, Philosopher and Mathematician.
Andrea Chilcote and Sara Burden, *Erik's Hope* (Arizona, Morningstar Ventures, Inc. 2012).

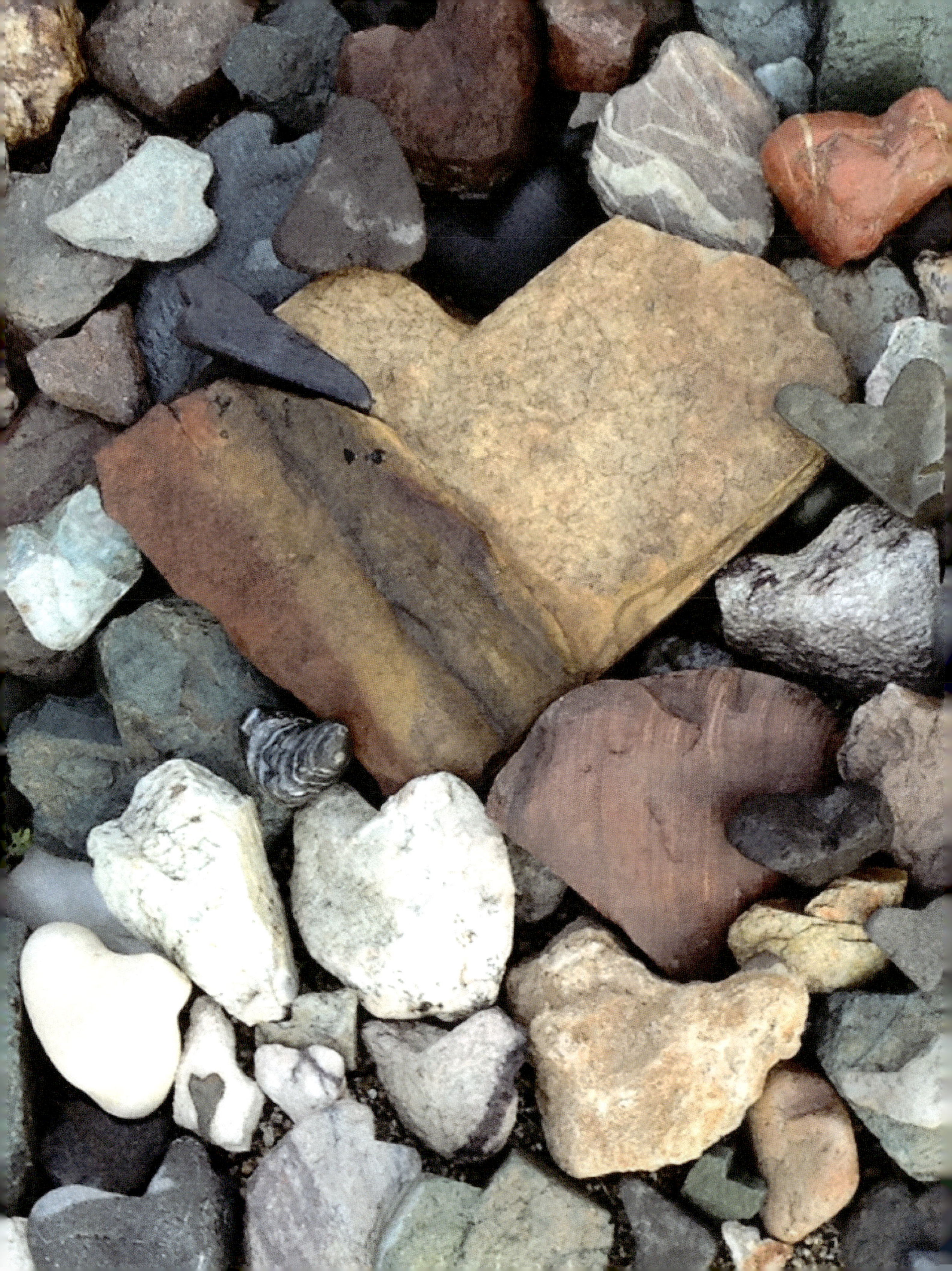

Made in the USA
Charleston, SC
20 November 2012